SOLITUDE'S SPELLBOOK

A BEGINNER'S GUIDE TO SOLITARY WITCHCRAFT

WILLOW DE WITTE

WILDERWORDS PUBLISHING

CONTENTS

INTRODUCTION

THE PATH OF THE SOLITARY WITCH

In the quiet interludes between the rustling leaves and the soft whispers of the wind, where the veil between the seen and the unseen is gossamer-thin, the solitary witch finds sanctuary. Here, beneath the silvery glow of the moon, the solitary witch embarks upon a profound journey—one of self-discovery, empowerment, and a dance with the mystical forces that weave through the fabric of existence. Welcome to the enchanting realm of solitary witchcraft, a path illuminated by the gentle luminescence of personal power, deep connection, and the magic found in the solitary spaces of the heart.

Section I: The Essence of Solitary Witchcraft

To walk the path of the solitary witch is to step into the shadows of solitude, where the bustling noise of the external world fades, and the soul's whispers become audible. Unlike the image of witches gathered in covens, solitary practitioners find solace and strength in the embrace of their own company. The essence of solitary witchcraft lies in the ability to find magic not in the external grandeur of elaborate ceremonies, but in the intimate, internal moments of communion with the mystical forces that surround us.

Imagine the path of the solitary witch as a labyrinth—a winding journey through the corridors of self-discovery, where every turn reveals hidden facets of the inner world. This labyrinth is not a maze of confusion, but a sacred journey where each twist and turn brings the practitioner closer to understanding the self and the cosmic dance in which they are an active participant. In solitude, the solitary witch navigates the labyrinth of their own consciousness, encountering challenges, embracing revelations, and uncovering the profound transformative power that lies within.

At the heart of solitary witchcraft is a deep attunement to the natural world—a recognition of the interconnectedness between the witch and the elements, the moon, and the stars. The solitary witch finds themselves amidst a symphony of nature and spirit, where the sacred and the mundane coalesce. This attunement is not a mere observation of nature but an active participation in the dance of creation, where the witch becomes a conductor, orchestrating spells and rituals that harmonize with the rhythms of the cosmos.

In the simplicity of sincere intention lies the true essence of solitary witchcraft. The solitary witch does not seek external validation or elaborate rituals to prove their power. Instead, they understand that the most potent magic arises from the purity of intent, from the authenticity of their connection to the unseen forces. Solitude becomes the crucible where intentions are refined, spells are woven with heartfelt purpose, and the simplicity of the sacred moment takes precedence over elaborate spectacle.

The tapestry of solitary witchcraft is woven in the silent moments of reflection, meditation, and communion with the sacred. It is a tapestry that reflects the unique journey of each practitioner—a visual representation of the spells cast, the lessons learned, and the evolution of the witch on their path. In the silence, the solitary witch finds the space to listen to the inner self, the echoes of ancient wisdom, and the subtle guidance of the unseen companions that accompany them on their journey.

Within the realm of solitary witchcraft, creativity knows no bounds. The solitary witch is free to explore eclectic paths, drawing inspiration from various traditions, mythologies, and firsthand experiences. This freedom is a defining feature of the solitary path, allowing the practitioner to adapt and evolve their practice organically. There are no rigid rules or dogmas; instead, the solitary witch is encouraged to embrace the fluidity of their craft, integrating elements that resonate with their soul's journey.

Nature, in all its myriad forms, becomes the teacher and guide of the solitary witch. The rustling leaves, the babbling brooks, and the silent majesty of ancient trees impart timeless wisdom to those who listen. The solitary witch learns to read the language of the natural world, interpreting the signs and symbols that guide their magical endeavors. Every stone, every plant, and every creature become a sacred messenger, offering insights into the profound interconnectedness of all life.

In solitude, the solitary witch discovers a kinship with the unseen—the spirits, deities, and energies that move between the worlds. These unseen companions are not distant entities but intimate allies, walking beside the witch on their magical journey. Solitude becomes a sacred space where communication with these companions is unhindered, and the veil between dimensions becomes permeable. The solitary witch learns to trust in the guidance of their unseen allies, fostering relationships that enrich and deepen their magical practice.

Section II: Embracing the Power Within

Embracing the power within is a cornerstone of solitary witchcraft. Unlike external sources of authority or validation, the solitary witch draws power from the inner cauldron—an infinite wellspring that resides within the core of their being. The cauldron is a vessel of transformation, where the mundane is transmuted into the magical, and intentions are stirred with the wand of the practitioner's will. In solitude, the solitary witch learns to tap into this inner cauldron, realizing that their power is not bestowed upon them but is an intrinsic aspect of their existence.

Central to the solitary path is the understanding of self-sovereignty—the recognition that each practitioner is the sovereign ruler of their own magical domain. Solitude provides the space for the solitary witch to define their own path, to set their own rules, and to govern their practice with a sense of autonomy. The sovereignty of self extends beyond the magical realm into the everyday, empowering the witch to navigate the complexities of life with confidence and resilience.

In the silent landscapes of solitude, intuition emerges as the North Star guiding the solitary witch through the vast expanse of magical possibilities. The intuitive faculties become finely tuned, serving as a compass that navigates the subtle energies, messages, and synchronicities encountered on the path. Solitude allows the solitary witch to listen to the whispers of intuition, trusting in the inner knowing that transcends logic and reason.

Solitude fosters a unique kind of magical resilience—an inner strength that allows the solitary witch to weather the storms of life and magic alike. The solitary practitioner learns to draw from the well of their own resilience, tapping into an unwavering source of determination and adaptability. In the face of challenges, the solitary witch stands firm, knowing that their magical practice is a sanctuary that can withstand the ebb and flow of life's tides.

Symbols, be they runes, sigils, or personal glyphs, become powerful conduits of intention for the solitary witch. In the quiet hours of solitude, the practitioner discovers the potency of personal symbols—codes that resonate with the deepest layers of their consciousness. These symbols are not arbitrary; instead, they are keys that unlock the doors to the inner realms, allowing the solitary witch to communicate with the subconscious, the higher self, and the forces that shape reality.

In solitude, the solitary witch becomes the architect of personal rituals—intimate ceremonies that are attuned to the rhythms of their own life. Personal rituals are not bound by tradition or expectation but are crafted with a sense of intention and purpose. Whether it's a daily meditation, a moonlit dance, or a simple offering to the sacred elements, personal rituals become a canvas upon which the solitary witch paints their magical expression.

Silence is a potent ally on the solitary path. In the stillness, the solitary witch discovers a sanctuary where thoughts crystallize, intentions gain clarity, and the magic of the unseen takes center stage. Solitude provides the space for the practitioner to commune with the silence, embracing it as a source of inspiration, insight, and a gateway to the realms beyond the veil.

While solitude is the chosen companion of the solitary witch, the dance with society adds another layer to the alchemical process of magical evolution. The solitary witch learns to navigate the delicate balance between the hermit's sanctuary and the interconnected web of human relationships. Solitude becomes a source of strength, allowing the practitioner to engage with society from a place of authenticity, wisdom, and a deep understanding of their magical sovereignty.

In solitude, dreams and reality intertwine, creating a tapestry that reflects the aspirations, visions, and manifestations of the solitary witch. The practitioner learns to walk between the worlds, where the boundary between waking and dreaming is porous. Solitude becomes a threshold, allowing the solitary witch to traverse the realms of dreams, visions, and waking life with equal reverence and awareness.

Solitude invites the solitary witch to confront the shadows that linger within the recesses of their psyche. These shadows are not adversaries but allies—guides that lead the practitioner to the deeper layers of their subconscious. Embracing the witch's shadow is a transformative act, allowing the practitioner to integrate the aspects of themselves that have long been concealed. Solitude becomes the canvas where the witch paints the colors of their own shadows, creating a masterpiece of self-awareness and healing.

Light and shadow are intertwined in the dance of the solitary witch. Solitude becomes a canvas where the practitioner paints with both light and shadow, acknowledging that each holds valuable lessons and insights. The solitary witch learns to find balance, understanding that the interplay of light and shadow is an intrinsic part of the magical journey. In solitude, the dance becomes a ritual, a continuous exploration of the dualities within and without.

The moon, with its ever-changing phases, becomes an enigmatic guide on the solitary path. Solitude allows the witch to attune to the lunar rhythms, harnessing the magic that flows with the waxing and waning of the moon. Whether it's the potent energy of the full moon or the quiet introspection of the new moon, the solitary witch learns to dance with the celestial body that illuminates the night sky, infusing their magic with lunar essence.

Night becomes a sacred sanctuary for the solitary witch, a time when the veil between worlds is thin, and the mystical energies are palpable. Solitude takes on a different hue beneath the moonlit sky, inviting the practitioner to engage in nocturnal rituals, dreamwork, and communing with the spirits of the night. The solitary witch becomes a nocturnal sorcerer, navigating the realms of shadow with confidence and reverence.

In solitude, the solitary witch discovers the alchemy of words and spells—a transformative process where intention is transmuted into reality. Whether written in a grimoire, spoken in ritual, or whispered to the wind, words become potent vessels of magic. Solitude provides the space for the practitioner to refine their language, to infuse their spells with sincerity, and to understand the resonance of every incantation cast into the cosmic cauldron.

In the quiet spaces of solitude, the solitary witch becomes attuned to the language of synchronicity—a subtle dance of signs and symbols that unfold in the tapestry of life. Every moment becomes a potential oracle, and every encounter holds a message from the unseen. Solitude allows the practitioner to listen with heightened awareness, recognizing the patterns that weave through the fabric of reality and guide them on their path.

Wild places—whether deep forests, secluded mountains, or untamed shores—become sacred sanctuaries for the solitary witch. In the solitude of these natural havens, the practitioner connects with the primal energies of the earth, forging a deep bond with the spirits of the land. The solitary witch becomes a guardian of these wild spaces, learning from the whispers of ancient trees, the murmurs of running water, and the primal heartbeat of the earth itself.

Solitude does not imply isolation. Instead, it becomes a web of connection that extends beyond the physical realm. In the silence, the solitary witch learns to communicate with other practitioners through the threads of energy that transcend time and space. Solitude becomes a meeting ground where the solitary witch can commune with kindred spirits, seek guidance from the wise ones who have walked before, and share the silent language of the magical community.

The path of the solitary witch is a journey of continuous becoming—a process of evolution, transformation, and self-discovery that unfolds with each step. In solitude, the witch learns that the journey is not a destination but a perpetual state of becoming. Solitude becomes a sacred space where the solitary witch can shed old skins, embrace new identities, and weave the threads of their magical self into a tapestry of endless possibilities.

Embracing the Enchantment of Solitude

As we embark on this exploration of solitary witchcraft, let these introductory reflections serve as a lantern, illuminating the vast landscapes of the solitary path. May the essence of solitary witchcraft, with its rich tapestry of self-discovery, empowerment, and connection with the mystical, become a guiding light on your journey. Embrace the power within, dance with the shadows, and may your solitude be an enchanting sanctuary where the magic of the unseen unfolds in wondrous and transformative ways. Welcome to the path of the solitary witch, where the whispering winds carry the secrets of the cosmos, and every step is a ritual in the dance of becoming.

CHAPTER ONE

UNDERSTANDING WITCHCRAFT

In the sacred silence of solitude, where the air is thick with the scent of herbs and the moon's glow illuminates hidden truths, the solitary witch begins their journey into the enchanting realm of witchcraft. This chapter serves as the gateway—a portal into the profound understanding of what it means to be a witch, the roots of this ancient practice, and the foundational principles that lay the groundwork for solitary witchcraft.

The Essence of Witchcraft

Witchcraft, often misunderstood and shrouded in mystery, is an ancient and multifaceted practice that spans cultures, continents, and centuries. At its core, witchcraft is the art of harnessing natural energies, working in harmony with the elements, and understanding the subtle forces that shape our reality. For the solitary witch, it is a personal journey of self-discovery, empowerment, and a deep connection with the mystical.

Defining Witchcraft

Witchcraft defies rigid definition, for it is a dynamic and ever-evolving practice. At its essence, witchcraft encompasses a range of magical traditions, spellcraft, and spiritual beliefs. The solitary witch embraces the fluidity of witchcraft, recognizing that it is a living, breathing entity that adapts to the needs, beliefs, and experiences of the practitioner.

The Witch as Practitioner

A witch is not defined by pointy hats, bubbling cauldrons, or black cats. The true essence of a witch lies in their role as a practitioner of magic—someone who taps into the unseen forces, channels natural energies, and crafts spells with intention. Whether in a bustling city apartment or a secluded forest dwelling, the solitary witch embodies the magic within, walking the path of the witch with authenticity and purpose.

Brief History of Witchcraft

Understanding the roots of witchcraft provides insight into its rich tapestry, woven with threads of folklore, persecution, and resilience. The history of witchcraft is a story of the human quest for spiritual connection, empowerment, and the preservation of ancient wisdom.

The origins of witchcraft are deeply entwined with the ancient practices of herbalism, divination, and shamanism. Across cultures and civilizations, individuals revered for their wisdom and magical abilities were the precursors to what we now understand as witches. These wise men and women, often healers and keepers of sacred knowledge, cultivated a deep connection with the natural world and the unseen energies that permeate it.

The Middle Ages saw a shift in perception, as societal attitudes towards magical practices evolved. With the rise of Christianity, the image of the witch became tarnished, associated with heresy and devil worship. The witch trials and persecutions that followed marked a dark period in history, during which countless individuals, predominantly women, faced accusations of witchcraft, leading to widespread fear and repression.

The 20th century witnessed a revival of interest in witchcraft, spurred by movements like Wicca and the resurgence of pagan traditions. Influential figures such as Gerald Gardner and Doreen Valiente played key roles in shaping modern witchcraft, introducing practices that celebrate nature, honor the divine feminine, and embrace the cycles of the moon. The solitary witch draws inspiration from these diverse traditions, weaving together a personalized tapestry of magical practices.

Dispelling Myths and Misconceptions

Witchcraft, surrounded by centuries of superstition and sensationalism, has endured a plethora of myths and misconceptions. Dispelling these misconceptions is crucial for the solitary witch to approach their craft with clarity and authenticity.

Myths portraying witches as malevolent beings with sinister intentions are deeply ingrained in cultural narratives. The solitary witch must recognize these stereotypes as fabrications and embrace the truth: witchcraft is a neutral practice, its essence shaped by the intentions and ethics of the practitioner. The path of the solitary witch is one of self-discovery, healing, and positive transformation.

The term "witchcraft" is often synonymous with the casting of spells and brewing of potions. While spellcraft is an integral aspect of witchcraft, it is essential to understand that the craft of the witch extends beyond the realm of magic. The solitary witch engages in a holistic practice that includes spiritual exploration, connection with nature, and the cultivation of intuitive abilities.

Contrary to popular belief, witchcraft is not a free-for-all pursuit lacking moral and ethical considerations. The solitary witch adheres to a personal code—an internal compass that guides their magical endeavors. Whether inspired by the Wiccan Rede or a set of individual principles, the witch's code emphasizes responsibility, harmlessness, and a harmonious relationship with the natural world.

Building a Magical Mindset

The foundation of witchcraft lies not only in the acquisition of practical skills but also in the cultivation of a magical mindset—a way of perceiving and interacting with the world that transcends the mundane.

The solitary witch embraces the idea that magic resides in the unseen, the intangible, and the mystical. This shift in perception opens the practitioner to a world of hidden forces, energies, and possibilities that elude the ordinary senses. Seeing the unseen is not about visualizing fantastical images but attuning the mind to the subtle currents of magical energy that flow through all things.

At the heart of witchcraft is the power of intention—a force that shapes the outcome of spells and rituals. The solitary witch understands that the energy behind their actions, thoughts, and words influences the manifestation of magical work. With a focused and clear intention, the practitioner channels their energy towards a specific goal, aligning with the fundamental principle that like attracts like.

Nature becomes the solitary witch's sacred guidebook, filled with symbols, rhythms, and cycles that mirror the ebbs and flows of magical energy. The phases of the moon, the changing seasons, and the cycles of the sun are not merely celestial occurrences but opportunities for the solitary witch to align their magic with the natural order. Embracing these cycles fosters a deeper connection with the forces that shape the universe.

In the elemental dance of earth, air, fire, and water, the solitary witch discovers profound allies. Each element carries unique energies, correspondences, and symbolic meanings that enrich the witch's magical practice. Developing a connection with the elements involves attuning to their qualities, understanding their influence, and incorporating their presence into spells, rituals, and daily life.

Intuition is the silent guide that whispers in the ear of the solitary witch. Cultivating intuitive wisdom involves tuning into the inner knowing, the gut feelings, and the subtle nudges that transcend rational thought. The solitary witch honors and trusts their intuitive abilities, recognizing them as invaluable tools for navigating the realms of magic and spirituality.

Embarking on the Solitary Path

The solitary witch embarks on a unique journey—one that is deeply personal, introspective, and laden with magical potential. While traditional witchcraft often involves communal practices within covens, the solitary path offers a distinct set of opportunities and challenges. Solitude becomes a canvas upon which the solitary witch paints their magical tapestry, weaving together influences, inspirations, and experiences into a rich and diverse practice.

Solitude is not a mere absence of company but a potent source of magical power. In the quiet moments of seclusion, the solitary witch finds the space to delve into the depths of their soul, to commune with the unseen forces, and to cultivate a profound connection with the natural world. Solitude becomes the crucible where the practitioner refines their magical skills, discovers hidden aspects of themselves, and forges a unique relationship with the mystical.

Freedom is a cornerstone of the solitary path. Unlike the structure of coven-based practices, the solitary witch has the freedom to explore diverse traditions, craft personalized rituals, and shape their magical identity without external constraints. This freedom invites the solitary witch to be an eclectic explorer, drawing inspiration from ancient traditions, modern practices, and personal experiences.

While the solitary path offers freedom and autonomy, it also presents its own set of challenges and rewards. Loneliness may arise, but in solitude, the solitary witch learns to find companionship in the unseen and the natural world. The rewards include the deepening of personal connection, the ability to tailor practices to individual needs, and the joy of witnessing the direct impact of magical workings.

The grimoire, or magical book, becomes an essential companion on the solitary witch's journey. It is not merely a record of spells and rituals but a living document that evolves with the practitioner. The solitary witch learns to create and maintain their grimoire, infusing it with personal insights, experiences, and the wisdom gained on their magical path.

Throughout history, there have been individuals who, whether by choice or circumstance, walked the solitary path of the witch. The solitary witch honors and draws inspiration from these predecessors, weaving their legacy into the fabric of their own practice. In the footsteps of cunning folk, hedge witches, and solitary practitioners of the past, the solitary witch discovers a kinship that transcends time.

Understanding witchcraft is not merely an intellectual pursuit but a prelude to the magic that unfolds when the solitary witch steps onto the enchanted path. In the chapters that follow, we will delve deeper into the practices, rituals, and reflections that form the essence of solitary witchcraft. Let this understanding of witchcraft be the lantern that guides you through the sacred corridors of your magical journey—a journey that is uniquely yours, steeped in the wisdom of the ancients and infused with the magic of the present. Welcome to the boundless realms of witchcraft, where every step is a dance, and every moment is an opportunity to embrace the enchantment of the solitary path.

Chapter Two

Embracing the Power Within

I n the sacred solitude of the witch's chamber, where the flickering candlelight casts shadows on ancient symbols, the solitary practitioner embarks on a journey of self-discovery and empowerment. This chapter delves into the core essence of solitary witchcraft—embracing the power within. It is a call to recognize the innate magic that resides in every individual, unlocking the doors to self-realization, personal sovereignty, and the transformative potential of the magical arts.

The Source of Power

As the solitary witch begins their journey, the first revelation lies in understanding the source of power that courses through their veins. It is not an external force to be sought outside the self, but a primal energy rooted deep within the essence of being.

In the heart of the witch, there exists an inner cauldron—an alchemical vessel where experiences, emotions, and intentions blend and simmer. This metaphorical cauldron is the crucible of transformation, where the raw elements of life are transmuted into the elixir of personal power. The solitary witch learns to tend to this inner cauldron, stirring its contents with intention, mindfulness, and an understanding of the magical potential within.

Personal energy and intent become the currency of witchcraft, and the solitary witch is the master of their own energetic landscape. Every thought, emotion, and action contributes to the energetic tapestry woven by the practitioner. Embracing the power within involves becoming conscious of this personal energy, directing it with intent, and recognizing its impact on the magical workings. Through awareness, the solitary witch learns to shape their reality by shaping their energy.

While personal power emanates from within, the solitary witch also recognizes their connection to the cosmic web of energy that interlaces the universe. This awareness opens avenues for tapping into universal forces, aligning with celestial energies, and co-creating with the greater tapestry of existence. The power within is not isolated but intertwined with the expansive threads of the cosmic dance.

The Essence of Self-Discovery

Embracing the power within is an act of self-discovery—a journey into the depths of the soul, where hidden facets are unveiled, and the true self emerges like a moonlit reflection on still waters.

Solitude becomes the mirror in which the solitary witch gazes upon the layers of their being. Self-reflection is a potent magical practice, allowing the practitioner to explore their beliefs, desires, fears, and potentials. In the quiet of solitude, the mirror reflects not only the physical form but also the echoes of the inner landscape, inviting the witch to embrace every nuance of their existence.

In the dance of light and shadow, the solitary witch acknowledges and embraces the shadows that linger within. These are not malevolent forces but aspects of the self that yearn for acknowledgment and integration. Embracing shadows is a courageous act, for in the shadows lie the keys to profound self-understanding and healing. The solitary witch learns to navigate the labyrinth of their own psyche, recognizing that every shadow has a story to tell.

Symbols are the language of the subconscious, and the solitary witch becomes a linguist of the soul. Through introspection and meditation, the practitioner unearths personal symbols that hold profound meaning and resonance. These symbols become potent tools in magical workings, serving as bridges between the conscious and subconscious realms. Whether it's a cherished animal, a recurring dream image, or a symbol from childhood, the solitary witch weaves these symbols into the fabric of their craft.

The Art of Self-Empowerment

To embrace the power within is to become a sovereign being, capable of navigating the currents of life with resilience, wisdom, and a deep sense of personal authority.

In the sacred space of solitude, the solitary witch cultivates self-confidence—a quality that stems from a profound trust in one's abilities and a belief in the inherent worthiness of the self. Magical workings are fueled by confidence, for it is the catalyst that propels intentions into the cosmic realm with unwavering certainty. Through affirmations, visualization, and acknowledging personal achievements, the solitary witch nurtures the flame of self-confidence.

Autonomy is the cornerstone of the solitary path. The solitary witch is not beholden to external authorities or dogmas but finds strength in personal sovereignty. Embracing the power within involves recognizing the right to make independent choices, set individual boundaries, and take full responsibility for one's magical journey. The solitary witch becomes the architect of their destiny, crafting a path that aligns with their authentic self.

Creativity is a magical force that flows from the wellspring of the soul. The solitary witch embraces their creative nature, whether through artistic expressions, writing, crafting, or other forms of creative endeavors. Creativity becomes a conduit for personal empowerment, allowing the practitioner to infuse their magical workings with the unique essence of their being. The act of creation becomes a sacred ritual, a manifestation of the power within.

Harmony with the Natural Self

To embrace the power within is to forge a harmonious relationship with the natural self—the unfiltered, authentic core that resonates with the rhythms of the earth and the whispers of the wind.

The solitary witch recognizes the inherent connection between personal cycles and the natural rhythms of the earth. From the waxing and waning of the moon to the changing seasons, the practitioner aligns their magical workings with the ebb and flow of natural energies. In this alignment, the power within becomes attuned to the greater dance of the cosmos, enhancing the efficacy of spells and rituals.

The body is a sacred vessel, and the solitary witch tends to its well-being with reverence. Embracing the power within involves nurturing both physical and spiritual aspects of the self. Through mindful practices such as meditation, energy work, and physical exercise, the witch ensures that their vessel is a receptive and vibrant channel for magical energies. Physical and spiritual well-being become intertwined threads in the tapestry of personal power.

Intuition is the compass that guides the solitary witch through the labyrinth of choices and possibilities. Embracing the power within involves trusting and cultivating intuitive wisdom. Whether making decisions in magical workings or navigating daily life, the practitioner listens to the quiet whispers of intuition, recognizing it as a source of profound guidance rooted in the depths of the self.

Rituals of Self-Empowerment

In the sacred space of solitude, the solitary witch crafts rituals that amplify the power within—ceremonies that celebrate the self, honor personal achievements and deepen the connection with the magical essence.

The solitary witch designs and performs rituals specifically dedicated to personal empowerment. These rituals may involve invocations of personal deities or archetypes, the charging of talismans symbolizing self-empowerment, and the crafting of spells aimed at fortifying the witch's inner strength. These ceremonies become milestones on the solitary path, marking moments of personal growth and transformation.

In the solitude of the magical chamber, the solitary witch takes time to celebrate milestones and achievements. Whether it's mastering a new spell, overcoming a personal challenge, or reaching a spiritual milestone, these moments are acknowledged with gratitude and reverence. Celebration becomes a form of magical expression, a recognition of the power within that propels the practitioner forward on their journey.

Under the silver glow of the moon, the solitary witch engages in moonlit affirmations—a practice that involves speaking affirmations aloud under the moon's radiance. This ritual not only strengthens the practitioner's connection with lunar energies but also infuses the spoken words with the potent energy of the moon. The solitary witch speaks words of self-empowerment, confidence, and manifestation into the nocturnal tapestry.

As the solitary witch delves into the exploration of embracing the power within, a radiant transformation occurs. Like the unveiling of a hidden gem, the practitioner discovers the luminous core of their being—an inner radiance that emanates with magical potential. In the chapters that follow, we will build upon this foundation, exploring the practical applications of the power within and delving into the art of crafting spells, rituals, and enchantments that resonate with the authentic self. Embrace the power within, dear solitary witch, for it is the key to unlocking the boundless magic that dwells in the sacred sanctuary of your soul.

Chapter Three

A Brief History of Witchcraft

In the tapestry of human history, the threads of witchcraft weave a complex and often misunderstood narrative. To embark on the path of solitary witchcraft is to step into a tradition that spans centuries, cultures, and continents. In this chapter, we will journey through the annals of time, unraveling the enigmatic history of witchcraft—a history fraught with persecution, resilience, and a profound connection to the mystical forces that shape the very fabric of existence.

Ancient Roots: The Seeds of Sorcery

Witchcraft's origins are deeply rooted in the ancient practices of our ancestors. Long before written records, individuals communed with the natural world, seeking to understand and harness its forces. These early practitioners, often known as cunning folk, shamans, or wise women and men, held a sacred role within their communities.

In prehistoric times, humans lived intimately connected to nature. The practices that would later be recognized as witchcraft were woven into the daily lives of our forebears. From herbal knowledge to divination, early humans relied on the wisdom of those who could navigate the unseen realms.

In the cradle of civilization, the ancient Egyptians and Mesopotamians cultivated intricate systems of magic. Priests and priestesses, versed in the art of ritual and spellcraft, communed with deities to ensure the prosperity of their societies. Magical texts, like the Egyptian Book of the Dead, offered guidance for the deceased on their journey to the afterlife.

The Hellenistic period ushered in a new era of magical exploration. The Greeks and Romans delved into theurgy, a form of ritual magic, to invoke the aid of deities and spirits. The philosopher-mystic Pythagoras and the renowned mage Apollonius of Tyana are among the figures who left their mark on the esoteric landscape of the time.

Medieval Marvels: The Witch in a Changing World

The medieval period witnessed a profound transformation in the perception of magic and those who practiced it. The rise of Christianity and shifting societal attitudes cast a shadow over the once-respected cunning folk, marking the beginning of a tumultuous chapter in the history of witchcraft.

Before the term "witch" acquired its negative connotations, cunning folk played vital roles in medieval communities. These wise men and women were sought after for their healing abilities, divinatory skills, and knowledge of herbal remedies. They were the custodians of ancient wisdom, passed down through generations.

As Christianity spread across Europe, it brought with it a new perspective on magic. Practices that were once integral to everyday life were now viewed with suspicion. The Church sought to consolidate power, and anything perceived as a challenge to its authority, including alternative spiritual practices, became a target.

In 1487, Heinrich Kramer and Jacob Sprenger, two German Dominicans, penned the Malleus Maleficarum (Hammer of Witches). This infamous treatise fueled the flames of the witch hunts that would sweep across Europe. It provided a blueprint for identifying, interrogating, and prosecuting those accused of witchcraft, perpetuating fear and paranoia.

The Witch Hunts: Darkness Descends

The late medieval and early modern periods marked a dark epoch for those accused of practicing witchcraft. The witch hunts, fueled by superstition, fear, and religious fervor, led to the persecution and execution of thousands.

From the 15th to the 18th century, Europe and colonial America were gripped by a wave of hysteria. The fear of witches reached its zenith, and any deviation from societal norms could lead to accusations. Old women, healers, and those living on the fringes of society often found themselves targets of suspicion.

Witch trials were grotesque spectacles, characterized by trials that were anything but just. Accusations were often based on hearsay and fueled by personal vendettas. The accused faced torture, and confessions were extracted through unimaginable cruelty. Many innocent lives were lost during this dark period.

The Pendle Witch Trials of 1612 in England are a notable example of the hysteria that swept through communities. Twelve individuals from the Pendle Forest area were accused and tried for witchcraft. Ten were found guilty and hanged. The trials exemplify the social and religious tensions that fueled the persecution of supposed witches.

Enlightenment and Evolution: Witches in a Changing World

The Age of Enlightenment in the 17th and 18th centuries brought about a shift in societal attitudes. As reason and science gained prominence, the witch hunts began to wane. The witch, once a symbol of fear, started to be romanticized and viewed through a different lens.

With the decline of the witch hunts, remnants of the cunning folk tradition persisted in the form of cunning women. These wise individuals continued to practice folk magic, providing healing, divination, and spiritual guidance. The transition from feared witches to respected healers reflected changing social dynamics.

The Romantic movement of the 19th century embraced the mystique of the witch. Folklorists and writers sought to preserve and romanticize the traditions of cunning folk, contributing to a cultural shift in how witches were perceived. Instead of being feared, they became figures of folklore and, in some cases, symbols of empowerment.

Modern Witchcraft: A Revival of the Craft

The 20th century witnessed a resurgence of interest in witchcraft, fueled by a longing for spiritual connection and a rejection of traditional religious structures. This period saw the emergence of modern witchcraft, often referred to as Wicca, and the popularization of alternative spiritual practices.

In the mid-20th century, Gerald Gardner introduced Wicca to the public. This modern form of witchcraft drew inspiration from folk traditions, ceremonial magic, and elements of the occult. Wicca emphasized nature worship, the celebration of the Sabbats, and the use of ritual tools. It gained popularity and diversified into various traditions and practices.

The feminist movement of the 1960s and 1970s played a significant role in the resurgence of interest in witchcraft. Wicca, with its emphasis on equality and reverence for the feminine divine, resonated with many women seeking spiritual empowerment. Diverse paths within modern witchcraft emerged, embracing a range of practices and traditions.

Solitary Witchcraft Today: Crafting the Path Alone

In the 21st century, the landscape of witchcraft is diverse and dynamic. Solitary witchcraft, in particular, has gained popularity as individuals seek personal autonomy, freedom of practice, and a connection to the ancient roots of the craft.

Solitary witches today embrace the freedom to craft their own paths. Drawing from ancient traditions, Wicca, and a myriad of other influences, practitioners personalize their rituals, spells, and magical workings. The emphasis is on autonomy, authenticity, and a deep connection to the self.

The advent of the internet has transformed the way witches connect and share knowledge. Online platforms, forums, and social media have created a global community of practitioners. Solitary witches can now exchange ideas, seek guidance, and find inspiration from a diverse array of perspectives.

Modern solitary witchcraft is characterized by eclecticism. Practitioners draw inspiration from various traditions, cultural practices, and personal experiences. There is an emphasis on inclusivity, recognizing that the path of the solitary witch is as diverse as the individuals who walk it.

The history of witchcraft is a tapestry woven with threads of resilience, persecution, and the eternal pursuit of the mystical. From the cunning folk of ancient times to the eclectic solitaries of the present day, the craft has endured, transformed, and adapted. As a solitary witch, you stand at the crossroads of this rich history, ready to weave your own thread into the ever-unfolding saga of witchcraft. In the chapters that follow, we will delve into the practical aspects of solitary witchcraft, drawing inspiration from the ancient roots and diverse branches of the craft as you embark on your unique journey.

Chapter Four

Myths and Misconceptions of Witchcraft

In the vast expanse of human imagination, witchcraft often finds itself entangled in a web of myths and misconceptions. From the cackling hags in pointy hats to malevolent spellcasters seeking to do harm, these portrayals have shaped public perception for centuries. As you embark on your journey into solitary witchcraft, it's imperative to unravel the threads of fiction from the authentic tapestry of the craft. This chapter aims to dispel common myths and offer a more nuanced understanding of what it means to practice witchcraft in the modern world.

Myth 1: Witches Are Evil and Malevolent

One of the enduring stereotypes surrounding witches is the belief that they are inherently evil and seek to harm others. This notion has roots in historical witch hunts, where individuals accused of practicing witchcraft were often depicted as agents of malevolence. In reality, witchcraft is a diverse and personal practice that encompasses a wide range of ethical perspectives.

Reality: The Ethical Spectrum of Witchcraft

Witchcraft, including solitary practices, spans a spectrum of ethical considerations. While some practitioners may engage in protective magic or spellwork aimed at justice, the majority adhere to principles of harm none, emphasizing a harmonious relationship with the natural world and fellow beings. Solitary witches, in particular, often focus on personal growth, positive transformation, and the pursuit of spiritual enlightenment.

Myth 2: Witches Worship the Devil

The association between witchcraft and devil worship is a pervasive myth that can be traced back to the witch trials of the medieval and early modern periods. Accusations of consorting with the devil were often used as a justification for the persecution of individuals practicing folk magic or alternative spiritual traditions.

Reality: Diverse Spiritual Beliefs

Modern witchcraft is not a monolithic practice, and beliefs about deities or higher powers vary widely among practitioners. Many witches, including solitaries, embrace polytheistic, pantheistic, or animistic perspectives. The concept of the devil is rooted in Christian theology, and while some witches may incorporate aspects of Christian mysticism, the majority do not adhere to a devil-centric worldview.

Myth 3: Witches Can Fly on Brooms and Cast Spells for Instant Gratification

The image of a witch soaring through the night sky on a broomstick is a popular trope in folklore and media. Likewise, the idea that witches can cast spells for instant gratification or wield magical powers effortlessly contributes to a skewed perception of the craft.

Reality: Symbolism and Practical Magic

The image of flying on broomsticks is symbolic and rooted in historical misinterpretations. In reality, broomsticks were associated with fertility rites and herbal practices. The casting of spells in witchcraft involves focused intention, energy work, and often requires time and dedication. Magic, whether performed by solitary witches or those in covens, is a deliberate and nuanced practice that emphasizes the interconnectedness of the practitioner with the energies they seek to manipulate.

Myth 4: Witches Are Solitary Isolationists Who Shun Society

Another misconception suggests that witches, particularly solitary practitioners, are reclusive individuals who shun societal interactions. This image may stem from the historical persecution of those practicing folk magic, as well as the portrayal of witches as outcasts in literature and media.

Reality: Diverse Social Engagement

Solitary witches, like their counterparts in covens, are not necessarily hermits or social outcasts. Many practitioners actively engage with their communities, pursue social justice causes, and build connections with like-minded individuals. The choice to practice solitary witchcraft often reflects a desire for personal autonomy rather than a rejection of social engagement.

Myth 5: Witches Can Control Others and Bend Them to Their Will

The notion that witches possess the power to control others, manipulate free will, or cast spells for personal gain is a persistent myth that contributes to the fear and mistrust associated with the craft.

Reality: Ethical Considerations and Personal Responsibility

Witchcraft places a strong emphasis on ethical considerations, and the majority of practitioners adhere to the principle of harm none. While spellwork may involve influencing circumstances, it is not a tool for coercion or manipulation. Solitary witches, in particular, often focus on personal responsibility and self-awareness, steering clear of practices that infringe upon the free will of others.

Myth 6: Witches Only Practice in Moonlit Forests and Candlelit Chambers

Popular imagery often portrays witches practicing their craft in moonlit forests, candlelit chambers, or mysterious and otherworldly settings. This romanticized view may contribute to the belief that such atmospheric conditions are prerequisites for effective magical workings.

Reality: Practicality and Adaptability

Witchcraft is a practical and adaptable craft that can be practiced in various settings. While some witches may find inspiration in natural settings, others may perform rituals in their homes, gardens, or urban environments. Solitary witches, in particular, often craft their practice around the resources and spaces available to them, emphasizing the adaptability of the craft to diverse settings.

Myth 7: Witches Are Only Women

A pervasive stereotype surrounding witches is the notion that they are exclusively women. This stereotype is deeply rooted in historical biases and the association of witchcraft with the feminine divine.

Reality: Diverse Identities and Genders

Witchcraft is an inclusive practice that welcomes individuals of all genders and identities. While the historical persecution of witches often targeted women, the modern craft embraces diversity. Men, non-binary individuals, and people of all gender expressions actively participate in witchcraft, challenging and dismantling the stereotype that witches are exclusively female.

Myth 8: Witchcraft is Inherently Dark or Light

The dichotomy of dark and light magic is a simplistic perspective that oversimplifies the complexities of witchcraft. This myth suggests that all practitioners fall into either benevolent or malevolent categories based on their magical workings.

Reality: Nuanced Perspectives and Intentions

Witchcraft is inherently nuanced, and practitioners recognize the gray areas that exist between simplistic notions of dark and light magic. The ethical considerations of spellwork are often determined by the intentions and motivations behind the magical workings. Solitary witches, in particular, may navigate a spectrum of magical practices, incorporating elements of both shadow and light in their craft.

Myth 9: Witchcraft Is Inherently Secretive and Exclusive

A prevailing misconception surrounding witchcraft is that it is a secretive and exclusive practice, shrouded in mystery and hidden from the uninitiated.

Reality: Accessibility and Openness

While some aspects of the craft may be kept private by individual practitioners, modern witchcraft has become increasingly accessible and open. Many witches, including solitaries, share their knowledge through books, online platforms, and community events. The emphasis on inclusivity and openness has demystified witchcraft, inviting newcomers to explore and learn.

Myth 10: Witches Possess Supernatural Powers

The idea that witches possess supernatural powers beyond the capabilities of ordinary individuals contributes to the mystique and fear surrounding the craft.

Reality: Natural Abilities and Skill Development

Witches, whether practicing alone or in groups, do not possess supernatural powers. Instead, they hone and develop natural abilities, such as intuition, energy manipulation, and focused intention. The effectiveness of magical workings often stems from skill development, practice, and a deep understanding of the interconnectedness of the universe.

Navigating the Realms of Reality

As you delve into the expansive realms of solitary witchcraft, it becomes crucial to navigate through the myths and misconceptions that surround the craft. The reality of witchcraft is diverse, ethical, and deeply rooted in personal exploration and connection with the mystical forces of the universe. By dispelling these common misconceptions, you can approach your practice with a clearer understanding, allowing the authentic essence of the craft to guide you on your solitary journey. In the chapters that follow, we will continue to explore the practical aspects of solitary witchcraft, building upon a foundation of knowledge and dispelling further myths that may arise along the way.

Chapter Five

The Basics of Magic

In the realm of solitary witchcraft, understanding the fundamentals of magic is akin to laying the cornerstone of your mystical journey. Magic, often spelled as magick to distinguish it from stage illusion, is the art of influencing and connecting with the energies that flow through the universe. In this chapter, we will delve into the basics of magic, providing you with the foundational knowledge to commence your exploration into the unseen realms and unleash the potential within.

Understanding Magic: A Primal Force

Magic is not an elusive or supernatural force reserved for a select few; rather, it is a primal and inherent aspect of existence. At its core, magic operates on the principle that everything in the universe is interconnected, and through focused intention and energy manipulation, practitioners can affect change by their will.

Magic is not bound by rigid rules or dogma; it is a fluid and adaptable force. Solitary witches often emphasize the personal and intuitive aspects of magic, allowing each practitioner to develop their unique style. The essence of magic lies in the relationship between the practitioner and the energies they seek to harness.

Central to the practice of magic is intent—the clear and focused desire for a specific outcome. Your willpower serves as the driving force behind your magical workings. As a solitary witch, you have the autonomy to set your intentions and wield your will in alignment with your personal ethics and values.

The Magical Practitioner: Connecting with Energies

Before delving into spellwork and rituals, it is crucial to understand your role as a magical practitioner and how to attune yourself to the energies surrounding you.

Grounding and centering are foundational techniques that establish a stable connection between yourself and the energies of the earth. Picture yourself rooted like a tree, drawing upon the energies of the earth's core. This practice helps balance your energy and provides a solid foundation for magical work.

Before engaging in magical workings, it is beneficial to cleanse and purify both yourself and your magical space. This can be achieved through various methods, such as smudging with herbs like sage or using consecrated water. Cleansing rituals remove any residual energies that may interfere with your magical intentions.

Creating a dedicated magical space, whether a small altar or an entire room, establishes a focal point for your practice. This space serves as a reflection of your magical identity and a place where you can amplify your intentions. Personalize it with symbols, crystals, and items that resonate with you.

The Elements: Building Blocks of Magic

In many magical traditions, the elements—earth, air, fire, and water—play a central role. Understanding their correspondences and harnessing their energies can enhance the potency of your magical workings.

Earth: Stability and Manifestation

Associated with the physical realm, earth represents stability, grounding, and manifestation. Crystals, stones, and herbs are often aligned with this element. When working with earth energies, focus on grounding your intentions and bringing your desires into tangible reality.

Air: Intellect and Communication

Air symbolizes intellect, communication, and the power of the mind. Incense, feathers, and written words are linked to the element of air. Use air energies to enhance mental clarity, communication skills, and the transmission of your intentions to the universe.

Fire: Transformation and Energy

The element of fire embodies transformation, passion, and the spark of energy. Candles, bonfires, and spices are aligned with fire. When incorporating fire into your magic, visualize the transformative power it brings, turning intentions into reality and igniting the energy within.

Water: Intuition and Emotion

Water symbolizes intuition, emotion, and the subconscious mind. Sea salt, shells, and bowls of water are associated with this element. Engage with water energies to enhance your emotional intelligence, connect with your intuitive side, and evoke the fluid nature of magic.

Tools of the Trade: Ritual Instruments and Symbols

While magic can be practiced with minimal tools, many witches choose to work with specific instruments and symbols to amplify their intentions and create a sacred space.

Athame: Symbol of Willpower

The athame, a ritual dagger, represents the willpower and intention of the practitioner. It is often used to direct energy during rituals and spellwork. Choose an athame that resonates with you, and dedicate it to your magical practice.

Wand: Channeling Energy

Wands serve as conduits for energy, helping practitioners direct and focus their intent. Craft a wand from natural materials or find one that speaks to you. Use it to draw symbols, cast circles, and channel energy in your magical workings.

Cauldron: Symbol of Transformation

The cauldron is a potent symbol of transformation and rebirth. It is used for mixing magical ingredients, burning herbs, and performing rituals. Incorporate a cauldron into your magical space as a representation of the transformative power of your craft.

Tarot and Divination Tools

Tarot cards, runes, or other divination tools can be valuable assets in a solitary witch's toolkit. These instruments offer insights, guidance, and a deeper connection to the mystical forces that surround us. Dedicate time to learn and understand the symbolism of your chosen divination method.

The Power of Words: Incantations and Spellwork

Words hold immense power in the practice of magic. Whether spoken aloud or written, incantations and spells serve as the vehicles through which your intentions are conveyed to the universe.

Crafting incantations involves selecting words that resonate with your intent and weaving them into a rhythmic and powerful expression. Use language that evokes emotion and aligns with the energy you wish to manifest. Speak or chant your incantations with confidence and conviction.

Spellwork encompasses a diverse range of techniques, from candle magic to jar spells. Choose methods that align with your preferences and intentions. Experiment with different spellwork techniques to discover what resonates most strongly with your personal magical style.

Aligning your magical workings with the phases of the moon adds an extra layer of potency. The waxing moon is ideal for spells of growth and manifestation, while the waning moon is conducive to banishing or releasing rituals. Consider the lunar cycle when planning your magical endeavors.

Energy Work: Channeling and Manipulating Energies

A fundamental skill for any magical practitioner, energy work involves the ability to sense, channel, and manipulate the subtle energies that permeate the universe.

Developing the ability to sense energy is crucial for effective magical work. Begin by focusing on your own energy and gradually expand your awareness to the energies in your surroundings. Pay attention to sensations, temperature changes, or vibrations.

Raising and directing energy involves generating a potent force and directing it toward a specific intention. This can be achieved through visualization, movement, or focused breathwork. Experiment with different techniques to discover the methods that resonate most strongly with you.

Before using magical tools or conducting rituals, it's essential to charge and cleanse them. Channel your energy into the tools, infusing them with your intent and purpose. Likewise, cleanse them of any residual energies that may interfere with your magical workings.

Embarking on Your Magical Journey

As you delve into the basics of magic, remember that your journey as a solitary witch is uniquely yours. These foundational principles provide a sturdy scaffold upon which to build your practice, but the true magic lies in your connection with the energies that flow through the universe. In the chapters that follow, we will explore specific magical techniques, rituals, and the ongoing development of your solitary witchcraft. Embrace the power within, trust your intuition, and step boldly into the enchanting realm of magic that awaits you.

Chapter Six

Defining Magic and Spellcraft

In the heart of solitary witchcraft lies the profound understanding of magic and spellcraft—the transformative forces that weave the fabric of the mystical journey you've embarked upon. In this chapter, we will delve into the essence of magic, explore the art of spellcraft, and unravel the threads that connect the solitary witch to the vast tapestry of the unseen realms.

The Essence of Magic: A Cosmic Dance

Magic is an intrinsic force that courses through the universe, connecting all living things in a cosmic dance of energy and intention. As a solitary witch, recognizing the essence of magic is the first step toward wielding its power.

At its core, magic operates on the principle that energies are interconnected. Everything in the universe vibrates with a unique energy signature, and through focused intention and manipulation, a solitary witch can tap into this vast reservoir of cosmic energy.

Intent is the catalyst that propels magic into action. Your willpower, focused through clear and specific intent, shapes the energy you

work with. As a solitary practitioner, your autonomy allows you to define your own magical goals, aligning them with your values, desires, and personal journey.

Spellcraft: Crafting Reality with Intention

Spellcraft is the art of shaping and directing magical energy to achieve a specific outcome. It is through spellcraft that a solitary witch becomes an active participant in the cosmic dance, molding reality in accordance with their will.

The Anatomy of a Spell

A spell is a structured and intentional ritual that harnesses magical energies to bring about a desired change. While the form of spells may vary, they typically include the following components:

- **Intent Statement:** Clearly define the purpose of your spell. Your intent statement should be specific, positive, and aligned with your ethical considerations.

- **Correspondences:** Choose correspondences such as colors, herbs, crystals, and symbols that resonate with your intent. These act as conduits for specific energies.

- **Visualization:** Envision the desired outcome with vivid detail. Visualization enhances your focus and connects your intention to the cosmic energies you are working with.

- **Incantation or Chant:** Craft a spoken or chanted rhyme that encapsulates your intent. The rhythmic flow of words adds potency to your spell.

- **Action or Gesture:** Incorporate a physical action or gesture to anchor your intent in the material world. This could be as simple as lighting a candle or more elaborate gestures, depending on the complexity of your spell.

Ethics in Spellcraft

Ethical considerations are paramount in spellcraft. As a solitary witch, you have the responsibility to ensure that your magical workings align with positive and constructive principles. Avoid spells that infringe upon the free will of others or are intended to cause harm.

Timing and Cosmic Alignments

The timing of spellwork can enhance its effectiveness. Many solitary witches choose to align their magical workings with specific cosmic cycles, such as the phases of the moon or astrological events. Consider the energetic influences of these celestial alignments to amplify the potency of your spells.

Types of Magic: From Practical to High Magic

Magic manifests in various forms, each serving a unique purpose in the repertoire of a solitary witch. Understanding these types of magic allows you to choose the most suitable approach for your intentions.

Practical Magic

Practical magic encompasses everyday spells and rituals that address immediate and tangible needs. This type of magic is well-suited for solitary witches seeking to manifest practical outcomes in their daily lives, such as prosperity, protection, or healing.

Ceremonial Magic

Ceremonial magic, often referred to as high magic, involves elaborate rituals and ceremonial practices. This type of magic is deeply rooted in symbolism, mysticism, and the invocation of spiritual entities. While it may require more preparation, ceremonial magic can be a transformative and profound experience for solitary practitioners.

Ritualistic Magic

Ritualistic magic involves the performance of rituals with specific symbolic actions and tools. These rituals create a sacred space and connect the practitioner to the energies being invoked. Solitary witches often develop personalized rituals that resonate with their unique spiritual path.

Folk Magic

Folk magic, also known as traditional or cultural magic, draws from the practices and beliefs of specific cultural or regional traditions. This type of magic often involves charms, talismans, and practices passed down through generations. Solitary witches can explore folk magic to connect with their heritage or explore diverse magical traditions.

Building a Spell: A Step-by-Step Guide

Crafting a spell is a deeply personal and intuitive process. While there is no one-size-fits-all approach, the following step-by-step guide can serve as a framework for building your own spells.

Step 1: Define Your Intent

Clearly articulate the purpose of your spell. What do you wish to manifest or transform in your life? Ensure your intent is positive, specific, and aligned with your ethical considerations.

Step 2: Choose Correspondence

Select correspondences that resonate with your intent. Consider colors, herbs, crystals, symbols, and any other elements that amplify the energy you wish to harness. Research and explore correspondences that align with your personal associations.

Step 3: Create a Sacred Space

Before casting your spell, create a sacred space. This can be a designated altar, a specific room, or any area cleansed and consecrated for magical workings. Ground and center yourself to establish a connection with the energies around you.

Step 4: Cast a Circle

Many solitary witches cast a circle to create a sacred and protected space for their spellwork. Visualize a sphere of light surrounding you, marking the boundary between the mundane and the magical.

Step 5: Perform the Ritual

Follow the components of your spell, incorporating the intent statement, correspondences, visualization, incantation or chant, and any physical actions or gestures. Engage with each element deliberately, focusing your energy on the manifestation of your intent.

Step 6: Release the Energy

Once the ritual is complete, release the raised energy into the universe. This can be done through visualization, symbolic gestures, or a spoken declaration. Trust that the cosmic energies will carry your intentions to the desired destination.

Step 7: Ground and Reflect

After releasing the energy, ground yourself by connecting with the energies of the earth. Reflect on the experience, acknowledging the work you have done and expressing gratitude to the forces that have assisted you.

Common Pitfalls in Spellcraft

While spellcraft is a powerful and transformative practice, there are common pitfalls that solitary witches may encounter. Awareness of these challenges can guide you toward more effective and ethically sound magical workings.

Lack of Clarity in Intent

Unclear intentions can result in ambiguous or undesired outcomes. Take the time to precisely define your intent before engaging in spellcraft. This clarity ensures that the energies you work with align with your true desires.

Neglecting Ethical Considerations

Ethics play a crucial role in spellcraft. Avoid spells that infringe upon the free will of others or cause harm. Regularly assess your magical practices to ensure they align with positive and constructive principles.

Overreliance on External Tools

While tools and correspondences can enhance spellwork, overreliance on external instruments may overshadow the power within. Remember that your intent, willpower, and connection to cosmic energies are the driving forces behind effective spellcraft.

Impatience and Unrealistic Expectations

Magic operates within the flow of cosmic time, and outcomes may not manifest instantly. Be patient and realistic in your expectations. Trust the process and remain open to the subtle ways in which magic unfolds.

Embracing the Alchemy of Magic

As you delve into the realms of defining magic and spellcraft, remember that the essence of your practice lies in the alchemy of transformation. Magic is not merely a set of techniques; it is a dynamic and reciprocal relationship between the solitary witch and the cosmic energies that dance through the universe. In the chapters that follow, we will explore specific spells, rituals, and further nuances of your solitary witchcraft journey. Embrace the alchemy within, trust in your magical abilities, and continue to weave the threads of your mystical tapestry with intention and reverence.

Chapter Seven

Building a Magical Mindset

In the tapestry of solitary witchcraft, the threads of practice are intricately woven with the fabric of mindset. As a solitary witch, cultivating a magical mindset is not merely a philosophical pursuit but an essential aspect that shapes the very essence of your craft. In this chapter, we will explore the transformative power of mindset, understanding the beliefs that underpin your magical journey, and unlocking the potential within.

The Power of Belief: Foundations of Magical Mindset

At the heart of solitary witchcraft lies the recognition that belief is a potent force, shaping reality in ways both subtle and profound. Your beliefs form the foundation upon which your magical practice stands, influencing the energies you attract and the outcomes you manifest.

Belief is the catalyst that propels magic into action. When you wholeheartedly believe in the potency of your spells, rituals, and the interconnected energies of the universe, you create a resonance that magnifies the effectiveness of your magical workings.

Challenge and expand limiting beliefs that may hinder your magical potential. These beliefs may be inherited from societal conditioning, personal experiences, or cultural narratives. By acknowledging and expanding beyond these limitations, you open yourself to a broader spectrum of magical possibilities.

Cultivating a Magical Mindset: Key Principles

Building a magical mindset involves embracing key principles that align with the transformative nature of solitary witchcraft. These principles serve as guideposts, shaping your perspective and influencing the energies you engage with.

- **Interconnectedness of All Things**: At the core of a magical mindset is the understanding that all things in the universe are interconnected. Every living being, every element, and every thought vibrates with energy, creating a cosmic web that binds the fabric of existence. Embracing this interconnectedness allows you to tap into the vast reservoir of universal energy.

- **Fluidity and Adaptability**: Magic thrives in a state of fluidity and adaptability. Cultivate a mindset that is open to change, flexible in approach, and receptive to the unexpected twists of the magical journey. Recognize that the only constant in the universe is change, and your ability to flow with these currents enhances your magical prowess.

- **Personal Responsibility**: A magical mindset is grounded in personal responsibility. Acknowledge that you are the architect of your reality and that the consequences of your magical workings are shaped by your intent and actions. Embrace the ethical considerations of solitary witchcraft, understanding the impact of your choices on yourself and the interconnected web of existence.

- **Imagination and Visualization**: Imagination is the fertile ground from which magic springs forth. Cultivate a vibrant imagination that allows you to visualize your intentions with vivid detail. Visualization is not a mere mental exercise but a powerful technique that bridges the gap between the ethereal and the material, bringing your magical goals closer to manifestation.

- **Patience and Trust in the Process**: Magic operates within the ebb and flow of cosmic time, and outcomes may unfold in ways beyond immediate comprehension. Develop the patience to trust in the process, understanding that the energies you set in motion will manifest at their own pace. Trust in the unseen forces that work in tandem with your intentions.

- **Connection with Nature**: Nature is both a teacher and a mirror for the solitary witch. Cultivate a mindset that honors the rhythms of the natural world, recognizing the cycles of the moon, the changing seasons, and the elemental forces that shape the landscape. A deep connection with nature enhances your attunement to the cosmic energies that flow through all living things.

Mindful Awareness: Navigating the Inner Landscape

Building a magical mindset requires mindful awareness, a practice that involves navigating the inner landscape of thoughts, emotions, and energies. Mindfulness is not about eradicating thoughts but observing them with non-judgmental awareness. As a solitary witch, cultivating mindful awareness enhances your ability to harness and direct the energies of your magical mindset.

Observing Thought Patterns: Take time to observe your thought patterns and identify any recurring beliefs that may influence your magical mindset. Are there self-limiting thoughts or doubts that arise when you engage in spellwork? By recognizing these patterns, you can consciously shift your mindset toward empowering beliefs.

Embracing Emotions as Energy: Emotions are potent energies that can fuel or hinder magical workings. Mindful awareness allows you to embrace emotions as dynamic energies that shape your magical intentions. Instead of suppressing or being overwhelmed by emotions, channel their energy toward your desired outcomes.

Energetic Alignment through Meditation: Meditation is a powerful tool for cultivating mindful awareness and aligning with the energies of your magical mindset. During meditation, focus on your breath, visualize your intentions, and attune yourself to the subtle currents of energy within and around you. Regular meditation enhances your ability to enter a magical state of consciousness.

Affirmations and Mindset Shifting: Crafting Your Reality

Affirmations are concise, positive statements that affirm your beliefs and intentions. Crafting and reciting affirmations is a transformative practice that shapes your mindset and influences the energies you attract.

Crafting Empowering Affirmations: Create affirmations that reflect the magical mindset you wish to embody. These statements should be positive, present tense, and aligned with your intentions. For example:

- "I am a channel for the cosmic energies that shape my reality."

- "My magical intentions manifest with ease and grace."

- "I trust in the process, knowing that the universe conspires in my favor."

Consistent Affirmation Practice: Incorporate affirmations into your daily routine. Repeat them during meditation, incorporate them into your morning or evening rituals, or place them in areas where you frequently spend time. Consistent affirmation practice reinforces your magical mindset and gradually shifts ingrained beliefs.

The Role of Symbols and Sigils: Gateways to the Subconscious

Symbols and sigils are potent gateways to the subconscious mind, serving as keys that unlock the mystical potential within. As a solitary witch, integrating symbols and sigils into your mindset can deepen your connection with the cosmic energies you seek to harness.

Selecting Personal Symbols: Identify symbols that resonate with your magical intentions and beliefs. These symbols can be drawn from cultural, mystical, or personal sources. Choose images that evoke a strong emotional response and align with the energies you wish to manifest.

Crafting and Charging Sigils: Sigils are symbolic representations of intentions that are charged with magical energy. Craft your own sigils by combining and simplifying the symbols that resonate with your goals. Once created, charge the sigils through focused intent, visualization, and energy work. Use them in rituals, meditation, or as talismans to reinforce your magical mindset.

Navigating Doubt and Skepticism: Strengthening Your Resolve

As a solitary witch, you may encounter doubt and skepticism, either from within or external sources. Navigating these challenges requires a resilient mindset that stands firm in the face of uncertainty.

Internal Doubt: Self-Reflection and Affirmation: When doubt arises within, engage in self-reflection to identify the root causes. Are there underlying beliefs or past experiences contributing to doubt? Counteract internal doubt with affirmations that reinforce your magical mindset. Remind yourself of the transformative experiences you've encountered on your journey.

External Skepticism: Confidence and Education: External skepticism may come from well-meaning friends, family, or societal influences. Approach skepticism with confidence and a willingness to educate others about your beliefs. Share your experiences, knowledge, and the positive impact of your magical practice. Remember that your journey is unique, and the proof of its validity lies in your personal experiences.

Enchanting Your Reality with a Magical Mindset

As you delve into the realm of building a magical mindset, remember that the mind is a potent cauldron of transformation. Your beliefs, thoughts, and emotions are the alchemical ingredients that shape the reality you experience. Cultivate a mindset that resonates with the magical principles of interconnectedness, fluidity, and personal responsibility. In the chapters that follow, we will continue to explore practical applications of your magical mindset, including spells, rituals, and the ongoing evolution of your solitary witchcraft journey. Embrace the enchanting potential within your mind, and continue to weave the threads of magic into the fabric of your existence with intention, mindfulness, and reverence.

Chapter Eight

Creating Your Sacred Space

In the practice of solitary witchcraft, the concept of sacred space holds profound significance. It is within this consecrated realm that the solitary witch engages with the energies of the universe, conducts rituals, and communes with the mystical forces that shape their magical journey. In this chapter, we will explore the art of creating your sacred space—an intimate haven where the veil between the mundane and the magical is thin, and the energies flow in harmony with your intentions.

The Significance of Sacred Space

A sacred space is a focal point for magical workings and spiritual practices. It serves as a sanctuary where the solitary witch can attune themselves to the energies of the universe, conduct rituals, and connect with their inner self. The creation of a sacred space is a personal and transformative act, aligning the physical environment with the intentions of the practitioner.

Elements of a Sacred Space

- **Altar:** At the heart of your sacred space lies the altar, a dedicated surface where you arrange tools, symbols, and items of personal significance. The altar becomes a focal point for your magical workings, a place where intention is magnified and cosmic energies are harnessed.

- **Candles:** Candles, with their flickering flames, are potent symbols of transformation and illumination. They can represent the elements, specific energies, or serve as conduits for focusing intention during rituals.

- **Crystals:** Crystals hold unique energies and vibrations. Select crystals that resonate with your magical goals and arrange them on your altar to enhance the energetic ambiance of your sacred space.

- **Herbs and Incense:** The aroma of herbs and incense can purify and consecrate your sacred space. Choose herbs and scents that align with your intentions and preferences, creating a sensory experience that enhances your magical practice.

- **Symbols and Sigils:** Incorporate symbols and sigils that hold personal significance or relate to your magical goals. These symbols act as gateways to the subconscious, reinforcing your intentions and connecting you with mystical energies.

- **Personal Items:** Infuse your sacred space with personal items that hold sentimental or magical value. These could include heirlooms, photographs, or objects representing your journey and spiritual path.

Selecting a Sacred Space

Your sacred space can be established indoors or outdoors, depending on your living situation and personal preferences. If practicing indoors, choose a quiet and private area where you won't be easily disturbed. If practicing outdoors, select a spot in nature—a garden, a secluded corner of a park, or even a balcony.

Consider the energies of the space you choose. Is it peaceful and conducive to introspection? Does it allow you to connect with the natural elements? Trust your intuition when selecting or creating your sacred space.

Creating Your Outdoor Sacred Space

Harmonizing with Nature

If you choose to create your sacred space outdoors, the natural environment becomes an integral part of your practice. Here's how to harmonize with nature and establish an outdoor sacred space:

- **Choose a Natural Setting:** Select a quiet and secluded spot in nature, such as a garden, a wooded area, or a peaceful corner of a park. Ensure that the space resonates with a sense of tranquility.

- **Connect with the Elements:** Since you're already in nature, take advantage of the elements present. Feel the earth beneath you, listen to the rustle of leaves for air, bask in the warmth of sunlight for fire, and incorporate a small bowl of water for the water element.

- **Natural Altar Elements:** Use natural materials for your outdoor altar. Arrange stones, twigs, flowers, and leaves to represent the elements and create a connection with the environment.

- **Weather Considerations:** Be mindful of the weather and seasonal changes. Your outdoor sacred space can evolve with the natural cycles, embracing the different energies present during various times of the year.

Cleansing and Consecrating Outdoor Space

- **Connect with the Land:** Before setting up your outdoor sacred space, spend some time connecting with the land. Sit quietly, feel the energy of the earth beneath you, and express gratitude for the opportunity to work in harmony with nature.

- **Symbolic Cleansing:** Symbolically cleanse the space by sprinkling a bit of water, consecrated salt, or even flower petals to mark the boundaries of your sacred area. This not only cleanses but also defines the energetic space you are creating.

- **Elemental Blessing:** Invoke the elements by acknowledging each one with words or gestures. This can be a simple acknowledgment of their presence and a request for their blessings.

Maintaining and Enhancing Your Sacred Space

Regular Cleansing

Just as it's important to cleanse your sacred space before setting it up, regular maintenance is crucial to keep the energies flowing smoothly. Depending on the frequency of your magical workings and the energy of the space, perform cleansing rituals as needed.

- **Smudging:** Regularly smudge your sacred space with herbs or incense to clear any accumulated energies.

- **Sound Cleansing:** Use singing bowls, bells, or other sound tools to refresh the vibrational resonance of the space.

Energetic Alignment

- **Meditation and Visualization:** Spend time in meditation within your sacred space. Visualize the energy flowing harmoniously, infusing the space with vibrant, positive vibrations.

- **Energy Work:** Engage in energy work within your sacred space. This can include practices like grounding, centering, and directing energy toward specific intentions.

Adapting to Seasonal Changes

Your sacred space can evolve with the changing seasons, aligning your magical practice with the natural rhythms of the Earth.

- **Seasonal Decor:** Adjust the items on your altar to reflect the changing seasons. Use seasonal colors, symbols, and elements to attune your sacred space to the energy of each season.

- **Outdoor Rituals:** Embrace outdoor rituals that align with the characteristics of each season. Whether it's celebrating the growth of spring or the introspection of winter, adapt your practices to harmonize with nature.

The Living Tapestry of Your Sacred Space

As you embark on the journey of creating your sacred space, remember that it is a living tapestry—a dynamic reflection of your magical intentions and an ever-evolving realm where the energies of the universe intertwine with your own. Whether nestled indoors or enfolded by the embrace of nature, your sacred space is a sanctuary for self-discovery, magical exploration, and communion with the mystical forces that guide your solitary witchcraft journey. In the chapters that follow, we will delve deeper into the practical applications of your sacred space, exploring rituals, spells, and the profound connection between your inner world and the enchanting environment you've crafted with intention and reverence.

Chapter Nine

Setting Up an Altar

In the realm of solitary witchcraft, the altar serves as the beating heart of magical practice. It is a sacred space where intention is magnified, spells are cast, and the practitioner connects with the energies of the universe. In this chapter, we will explore the art of setting up an altar—a personal and symbolic space that acts as a bridge between the mundane and the mystical.

The Significance of the Altar

The altar holds profound significance in the practice of witchcraft. It is a physical representation of your magical intentions, a focal point for rituals, and a space where you can commune with the divine. Setting up an altar is a personal and transformative act, allowing you to infuse the space with your energy, intention, and connection to the mystical forces that guide your solitary witchcraft journey.

Elements of the Altar

An altar can be a simple tabletop or a dedicated surface that holds various tools, symbols, and items of personal significance. Each element on the altar contributes to the overall energy and purpose of the space.

The altar cloth serves as the foundation, representing the element of earth. Choose a cloth that resonates with your magical intentions, whether it's a solid color, a pattern, or a specific material.

Candles are symbolic of the element of fire and act as conduits for focusing intention during rituals. Select candles in colors that align with your magical goals. For example, red for passion, green for abundance, or white for purity.

Crystals, representing the element of earth, hold unique energies and vibrations. Choose crystals that resonate with your intentions and place them strategically on your altar to enhance the energetic ambiance.

Herbs and incense, representing the element of air, add a sensory dimension to your altar. Choose scents and herbs that align with your intentions, such as lavender for peace, sage for purification, or cinnamon for energy.

Symbols and sigils incorporated onto your altar resonate with your intentions. These can be drawn on paper, engraved on candles, or represented by physical objects. Arrange them in a way that feels visually balanced and meaningful.

Personal items, such as photographs or trinkets, can be placed on the altar to infuse it with personal meaning and connection to your journey.

Setting Up Your Altar

Selecting the Altar Space: Choose a dedicated space for your altar, whether it's a table, a shelf, or any flat surface. Consider factors like privacy, accessibility, and the energetic vibes of the space.

Cleansing the Altar Space: Before placing any items on the altar, cleanse the surface using smudging, sound cleansing, or any other preferred method. This ensures that the space is free from any lingering energies that may interfere with your magical workings.

Placing the Altar Cloth: Lay the altar cloth as the foundation of your magical space. The color and material of the cloth can be chosen based on your personal preferences and the correspondences associated with your magical goals.

Positioning Candles: Place candles on your altar, representing the element of fire. You may choose to use one central candle or several candles, each corresponding to a specific intention or element. Ensure they are secure and won't pose a fire hazard.

Arranging Crystals: Position crystals on your altar to represent the element of earth. Arrange them in a way that feels visually appealing and energetically aligned with your intentions. Crystals can also be charged with specific energies to amplify their magical properties.

Incorporating Herbs and Incense: Add herbs or incense to your altar to represent the element of air. Use a censer or a fireproof dish to burn herbs or incense safely. The aromatic scents will add an extra layer of sensory experience to your magical workings.

Integrating Symbols and Sigils: Incorporate symbols and sigils onto your altar that resonate with your intentions. These can be drawn on paper, engraved on candles, or represented by physical objects. Arrange them in a way that feels visually balanced and meaningful to you.

Infusing Personal Items: Place personal items on the altar that hold sentimental or magical value. These could include photographs, trinkets, or objects that represent your journey and spiritual path.

Practical Considerations for Your Altar

While setting up an altar is a deeply personal and intuitive process, there are practical considerations to keep in mind.

Space Constraints: If you have limited space, consider creating a portable or collapsible altar that can be easily assembled and disassembled. This allows you to practice witchcraft even in small living spaces.

Secrecy and Privacy: If privacy is a concern, especially in shared living spaces, choose a location for your altar that is discreet and can be easily concealed or transformed into a non-magical setup when necessary.

Maintenance: Regularly clean and maintain your altar space. Dusting, cleansing, and refreshing the items on your altar contribute to the overall vibrancy and effectiveness of your magical workings.

Adaptability: Your altar can evolve over time. Feel free to add, remove, or rearrange items based on changes in your spiritual practice, goals, or personal preferences. Let your altar grow and adapt with you.

Altar Dedication Ritual

Once your altar is set up, consider performing a dedication ritual to officially consecrate the space for magical workings. This ritual can be as elaborate or as simple as you desire, depending on your preferences.

- **Cleansing Ritual**: Begin by cleansing the altar space using smudging, sound cleansing, or any other method of your choice. This clears away any lingering energies and prepares the space for consecration.

- **Invocation of Elements**: Invoke the elements by acknowledging each one and inviting their energies to bless your altar. This can be done through words, gestures, or visualizations.

- **Personal Invocation**: Call upon the divine, deities, or energies that resonate with your practice. Share your intentions for the altar and seek their guidance and blessings.

- **Charging Ritual Tools**: If you have specific tools on your altar, such as a wand or athame, take a moment to individually charge and dedicate each tool. This can be done through visualization, passing the tool through the elements, or any other method that feels appropriate.

- **Affirmation of Purpose**: Clearly state your intentions for the altar. Affirm the purpose of the space, whether it's for spellwork, meditation, or communing with the divine. Speak from the heart and with conviction.

- **Offerings**: Consider making symbolic offerings to the elements or deities you've invoked. This can be as simple as placing a small bowl of water, a candle, or a bit of food on the altar. Express gratitude for the energies that will be present in your magical space.

- **Closing and Sealing**: Conclude the dedication ritual by thanking the elements, deities, or energies you've invoked. State that the ritual is complete and that the altar is now consecrated for your solitary witchcraft practice.

An example of such a ritual:

Altar Dedication

Ingredients:

- A representation of the four elements (earth, air, fire, water)

- A small dish of salt

- A feather or incense for air

- A candle for fire

- A bowl of water

Procedure:

Prepare Your Space:

Choose a quiet and undisturbed space where you can connect with the energies around you.

Set up your altar, placing the elemental representations in their respective corners.

Center Yourself:

Stand in the center of your sacred space, take a few deep breaths, and ground yourself. Feel the connection between your energy and the earth beneath.

Invoke the Elements:

Facing each direction, acknowledge and invite the energies of the elements.

- *"Spirits of Earth, stable and grounding, join me in this sacred space."*

- *"Spirits of Air, swift and free, bless this altar with your inspiration."*

- *"Spirits of Fire, passionate and transformative, infuse this space with your energy."*

- *"Spirits of Water, flowing and intuitive, cleanse and purify this sacred ground."*

Salt Blessing:

Take a pinch of salt and sprinkle it around your altar, creating a protective boundary.

- *"With this salt, I purify and protect this space. May only positivity enter and negativity be repelled."*

Incense or Feather Blessing:

Pass the incense or feather through the air around your altar.

- *"By the breath of air, may inspiration and clarity fill this space. Let my intentions rise like smoke to the divine."*

Candle Lighting:

Light the candle and gaze into the flame.

- *"With the fire's light, I ignite the passion within. May this flame be a beacon of my magical journey."*

Water Blessing:

Dip your fingers into the bowl of water and gently sprinkle it on your altar.

- *"In the waters of intuition, may this altar be cleansed and blessed. Flowing with the energy of the moon, the source of my magic."*

Personal Invocation:

Speak from your heart, expressing your personal dedication to the craft. Share your intentions and aspirations.

Closing:

Thank the elements for their presence and release the energies invoked.

- *"Spirits of Earth, Air, Fire, and Water, I thank you for gracing my altar. May this sacred space be a reflection of my magical journey. So mote it be."*

Seal the Space:

Close your ritual by envisioning a protective bubble around your sacred space. Feel the energies settle into a harmonious balance.

Altar Maintenance and Evolution

As you embark on your solitary witchcraft journey, your altar will become a dynamic reflection of your magical practice. Regular maintenance is crucial for keeping the energies flowing smoothly and ensuring that your altar remains a potent and sacred space.

Regular Cleansing:

- Smudging: Regularly smudge your altar with herbs or incense to clear any accumulated energies.

- Sound Cleansing: Use singing bowls, bells, or other sound tools to refresh the vibrational resonance of the altar.

Energetic Alignment:

- Meditation and Visualization: Spend time in meditation at your altar. Visualize the energy flowing harmoniously, infusing the space with vibrant, positive vibrations.

- Energy Work: Engage in energy work within the space of your altar. This can include practices like grounding, centering, and directing energy toward specific intentions.

Altar Evolution:

- Adapt to Changes: Your altar can evolve with your changing spiritual journey. Feel free to add or remove items based on shifts in your practice, goals, or personal preferences.

- Seasonal Adjustments: Consider making seasonal adjustments to your altar, incorporating elements and symbols that align with the energies of each season.

Your Personal Gateway to the Mystical

As your altar becomes the focal point of your solitary witchcraft practice, remember that it is more than a physical arrangement of items—it is a gateway to the mystical, a tangible representation of your magical intentions, and a sacred space where the energies of the universe converge with your own. In the chapters that follow, we will delve deeper into the practical applications of your altar, exploring rituals, spells, and the profound connection between your inner world and the enchanted realm you've crafted with intention and reverence.

Chapter Ten

Choosing and Cleansing Tools

In the journey of solitary witchcraft, the selection and care of your magical tools are pivotal steps on the path to harnessing the energies of the craft. These tools serve as extensions of your will, conduits for your intentions, and vessels for the manifestation of magical energy. In this chapter, we will explore the art of choosing your tools with intention and the importance of keeping them cleansed and attuned to your magical workings.

Choosing Your Tools with Intention

Selecting your magical tools is a deeply personal and reflective process. These tools become an integral part of your practice, aiding in your rituals, spells, and connection to the mystical energies. Here, we will delve into key considerations for choosing the primary tools used in solitary witchcraft.

Athame

The athame, a ritual dagger with a double-edged blade, holds immense significance in witchcraft. Traditionally associated with the element of air, the athame is a symbol of will and intention. When choosing an athame, focus on how it feels in your hand. The weight, balance, and material should resonate with you on an energetic level.

Consider the design and symbolism of the athame. Some practitioners prefer a simple, unadorned blade, while others choose a dagger with inscriptions, runes, or symbolic engravings. Your athame is a personal representation of your magical will, so let its appearance speak to your inner self.

Wand

The wand, often associated with the element of fire, is a tool of invocation and directing energy. When selecting a wand, consider the material, length, and craftsmanship. Wands can be crafted from various materials such as wood, metal, or crystal, each carrying its unique energy.

Allow yourself to be drawn to a wand that resonates with your energy. If possible, explore the energy of different wands before making your choice. Consider the significance of the wood or material used, as well as any decorative elements. Your wand is an extension of your magical self, so let it be a reflection of your inner power.

Chalice

The chalice, representing the element of water, is a vessel for holding liquids during rituals. It is often used to symbolize the divine feminine and the womb of creation. When choosing a chalice, pay attention to its size, shape, and material.

Consider how the chalice feels in your hands and the emotions it evokes. Some witches prefer a simple, unadorned chalice, while others choose one with intricate designs or symbols. As with all tools, let your intuition guide you. The chalice should feel like a sacred vessel, ready to hold the energies of your magical workings.

Pentacle

The pentacle, a five-pointed star enclosed in a circle, is a potent symbol of protection and manifestation. Associated with the element of earth, the pentacle is often used to consecrate and empower objects. When selecting a pentacle, focus on the design, material, and symbolism.

Choose a pentacle that resonates with your personal beliefs and intentions. Some witches prefer a traditional design, while others may opt for a more elaborate or modern interpretation. The material of the pentacle can range from metal to wood, each carrying its own energetic properties. Let the pentacle be a reflection of your connection to the earth and the energies you seek to harness.

Cauldron

The cauldron, often associated with the element of water or fire, is a symbol of transformation and rebirth. It is a versatile tool used for brewing potions, incense, and performing rituals. When choosing a cauldron, consider the size, material, and intended use.

Select a cauldron that suits your practical needs and resonates with your magical aesthetic. Some witches prefer cast iron cauldrons for their durability and connection to the earth, while others may choose a smaller, decorative cauldron for symbolic purposes. Your cauldron is a vessel of magical potential, so let its presence inspire your craft.

Selecting Additional Tools

Beyond the primary tools mentioned above, you may choose to incorporate other items into your practice, such as crystals, herbs, candles, and divination tools. Each of these items holds its own magical properties, and your selection should align with your intentions and the energies you wish to invoke.

When choosing crystals, consider their metaphysical properties and how they resonate with your goals. Research the correspondences of herbs and select those that align with your intentions for spellwork or rituals. Candles, with their colors and scents, can enhance the atmosphere and energy of your magical space. If you choose to include divination tools, such as tarot cards or runes, select a deck or set that speaks to your intuition.

Cleansing and Attuning Your Tools

Once you have chosen your magical tools, it is essential to cleanse and attune them to your energy. This process removes any residual energies from previous handling or manufacturing, allowing your tools to become a pure and potent extension of your magical self.

Cleansing Rituals

There are various methods for cleansing your magical tools, and the approach you choose may depend on the type of tool and your personal preferences. Some effective cleansing methods include:

Elemental Cleansing:

- **Air:** Pass the tool through incense smoke, symbolizing the element of air.

- **Water:** Gently wash the tool in consecrated water or leave it out during a rain shower.

- **Earth:** Bury the tool in soil or sprinkle it with salt to absorb any lingering energies.

- **Fire:** Pass the tool through the flame of a candle, symbolizing the element of fire.

Smudging:

- Use sacred herbs, such as sage or Palo Santo, to smudge the tool with purifying smoke. Pass the tool through the smoke, focusing on the intention of cleansing.

Visualization:

- Envision a stream of pure, white light flowing through the tool, cleansing away any energies that do not align with your own. Visualize the tool becoming a blank canvas ready to absorb your magical intentions.

Attuning Rituals

Once cleansed, it's time to attune your tools to your personal energy. This process aligns the tools with your magical intentions and creates a harmonious connection between you and the instrument.

Personal Connection:

- Hold each tool in your hands and spend some time meditating with it. Feel its energy and let it merge with your own. Establish a personal connection by imbuing the tool with your intentions and magical purpose.

Elemental Blessing:

- Invoke the elements corresponding to each tool (air for athame, fire for wand, water for chalice, earth for pentacle, and a combination for the cauldron). Hold the tool and visualize it being blessed by the respective elemental energy.

Moonlight or Sunlight Charging:

- Place your tools under the light of the moon or sun to charge them with celestial energy. The moon's energy is often associated with intuition and receptivity, while the sun's energy is linked to vitality and strength.

Intentional Use:

- Incorporate your tools into your magical workings. Use them in spells, rituals, or meditations to further attune them to your energy. The more you work with your tools, the stronger the connection becomes.

Storing and Respecting Your Tools

Once cleansed and attuned, it's crucial to store your magical tools with care and respect. Consider the following guidelines for storing and maintaining your tools:

Dedicated Space:

- Designate a specific space for your tools, whether it's a dedicated altar, a chest, or shelves. This creates a sacred and organized environment for your magical instruments.

Protection:

- Keep your tools protected from physical damage and external energies. Consider wrapping them in a consecrated cloth or placing them in individual bags.

Regular Cleansing:

- Periodically cleanse your tools, even if you're not actively using them. This helps maintain their purity and prevents the accumulation of stagnant energies.

Respectful Handling:

- Treat your tools with respect and reverence. Avoid allowing others to handle them without your permission, and use them mindfully in your magical workings.

Intuitive Adaptations:

- As your practice evolves, you may feel guided to adapt or add new tools. Trust your intuition and allow your toolkit to grow and evolve with your magical journey.

Empowering Your Craft with Sacred Tools

Choosing and cleansing your magical tools is a significant step on the solitary witch's journey. These instruments become extensions of your magical self, aiding in the manifestation of your intentions and the connection to the mystical energies that surround us. As you embark on this path, remember that the magic lies not only in the tools themselves but in the intention, respect, and personal connection you infuse into each one. In the chapters that follow, we will explore the practical applications of these tools, guiding you through rituals, spells, and the cultivation of your unique magical practice.

Chapter Eleven

Connecting with Elements and Energies

In the vibrant tapestry of solitary witchcraft, the fundamental connection with the elements and energies forms the very essence of our craft. As a solitary witch, your journey unfolds against the backdrop of nature's elements—earth, air, fire, water, and spirit. This chapter invites you to delve into the profound and transformative experience of connecting with these primal forces, weaving their energies into the fabric of your magical practice.

Embarking on Elemental Exploration

Each element carries its unique essence and symbolism, playing a crucial role in the balance and harmony of the natural world. As you embark on the exploration of the elements, consider the following insights into their significance and the ways you can forge a meaningful connection with each.

Earth: Foundation and Stability

The element of earth, grounded and steadfast, is the foundation upon which all magic stands. It embodies stability, fertility, and abundance. To connect with the energy of earth:

- **Commune with Nature:** Spend time in nature, whether it's a forest, park, or your own garden. Feel the earth beneath your feet and connect with its grounding energy.

- **Gardening:** Cultivate a small garden or tend to potted plants. Planting and nurturing life in the soil establishes a direct connection with the earth element.

- **Crystals and Gemstones:** Work with crystals and gemstones associated with earth, such as hematite, moss agate, or jasper. Hold them in your hands during meditation to absorb their grounding energy.

- **Practicality and Stability:** Embrace practical activities that ground you in the physical realm. Cooking, crafting, or organizing your living space can foster a sense of stability.

Air: Intellect and Communication

The element of air embodies intellect, communication, and the expansive realm of thought. It is the breath of life that carries both inspiration and clarity. To connect with the energy of air:

- **Breathwork:** Engage in mindful breathing exercises. Focus on the rhythm of your breath, allowing it to attune you to the subtle currents of air.

- **Wind Observations:** Spend time observing the wind. Whether it's a gentle breeze or a powerful gust, feel its energy and let it clear your mind.

- **Feathers and Birds:** Collect feathers or observe birds in flight. These symbols of air can serve as talismans, connecting you to the element's energy.

- **Intellectual Pursuits:** Stimulate your intellect through reading, writing, or engaging in thoughtful conversations. Air's energy encourages mental clarity and the exchange of ideas.

Fire: Transformation and Willpower

Fire, the element of transformation and willpower, possesses a dynamic and powerful energy. It represents both the spark of creation and the force of change. To connect with the energy of fire:

- **Candle Magic:** Engage in candle magic by lighting candles of different colors to correspond with your intentions. Focus on the flame and let its energy fuel your will.

- **Bonfires or Ritual Fires:** If circumstances allow, participate in bonfires or create ritual fires. The dancing flames serve as a direct connection to the transformative power of fire.

- **Sun Meditation:** Bask in the warmth of the sun during sunrise or sunset. Visualize its rays infusing you with vitality and empowering your inner flame.

- **Passion Projects:** Channel the energy of fire into projects that ignite your passion. Whether it's creative pursuits or personal goals, let the fire within propel you forward.

Water: Emotion and Intuition

Water, with its fluid and adaptable nature, represents emotion, intuition, and the ebb and flow of life. It is the source of purification and renewal. To connect with the energy of water:

- **Water Scrying:** Practice scrying with a bowl of water. Allow your gaze to soften as you peer into the depths, seeking insights and messages from the intuitive realm.

- **Moonlit Reflections:** Reflect near bodies of water, especially under the moonlight. The moon's connection with water amplifies the intuitive and emotional aspects of this element.

- **Cleansing Rituals:** Perform water-based cleansing rituals, such as ritual baths or consecrating tools in running water. Embrace the purifying essence of water to cleanse and renew.

- **Divination with Water:** Utilize water as a divination tool. Drop a small object into a bowl of water and observe the ripples for insights into your questions or concerns.

Spirit: Unity and Transcendence

The fifth element, often referred to as spirit or ether, transcends the physical elements and embodies the essence of unity and interconnectedness. It is the thread that weaves through all things. To connect with the energy of spirit:

- **Meditation and Contemplation:** Practice meditation and

contemplation to attune yourself to the transcendent energy of spirit. Explore the interconnectedness of all existence.

- **Connection to Higher Self:** Seek connection with your higher self through introspective practices. Journaling, soul-searching, and self-reflection can deepen your connection to the spiritual realm.

- **Sacred Space Dedication:** Dedicate a sacred space within your home or in nature to honor the element of spirit. Create an altar that represents your connection to the divine.

- **Rituals of Transcendence:** Engage in rituals that transcend the mundane and connect you with the divine. Whether through prayer, ritual dance, or chanting, let your spirit soar beyond the confines of the physical world.

Creating Elemental Harmony in Your Practice

As a solitary witch, integrating the elemental energies into your magical practice enhances the potency and depth of your workings. Consider weaving these elemental energies into your rituals, spells, and daily life to create a harmonious and balanced magical practice.

Elemental Rituals

Crafting elemental rituals allows you to attune to the energies of each element individually or in combination. These rituals can be adapted to suit your preferences, and the intention can range from seeking balance to invoking specific qualities associated with each element.

Balancing Ritual:

- Begin by standing or sitting in a comfortable position. Close your eyes and take a few deep breaths to center yourself. Visualize each element—earth, air, fire, water, and spirit—surrounding you in a circle. Feel the energies of each element merging with your own, creating a harmonious and balanced aura.

Elemental Invocation:

- Create an altar with representations of each element. Light a candle for fire, place a bowl of water, scatter earth or soil, and incorporate symbols of air. Invoke the energies of each element, expressing gratitude for their presence in your magical journey.

Elemental Meditation:

- Devote a meditation session to each element. Focus on the sensations, colors, and energies associated with earth, air, fire, water, and spirit. Let the qualities of each element permeate your being, fostering a deeper connection.

Elemental Spells

Integrating elemental energies into your spells amplifies their effectiveness and aligns them with the natural forces. Whether it's a spell for protection, manifestation, or healing, consider the elemental associations and how they can enhance your magical workings.

Earth Spell for Grounding:

- To ground and stabilize your energy, craft a spell using earth-associated elements. Use crystals like hematite, burn earthy incense, and incorporate soil or stones. Focus on your intention and the grounding energy of the earth element.

Air Spell for Clarity:

- Enhance mental clarity and communication with an air-inspired spell. Utilize incense, feathers, and the power of breath. As you perform the spell, visualize the cleansing and clarifying energy of air sweeping away mental fog.

Fire Spell for Transformation:

- Embrace the transformative power of fire in your spellwork. Use candles, symbolic representations of flames, and fiery herbs. Infuse your spell with the passion and energy of fire as you seek positive transformation.

Water Spell for Emotional Healing:

- Craft a spell for emotional healing using the soothing and purifying energy of water. Incorporate a bowl of consecrated water, use blue or silver candles, and include symbols associated with the flow of emotions. Allow the gentle energy of water to cleanse and renew.

Spiritual Spell for Connection:

- To deepen your spiritual connection, design a spell focused on the element of spirit. Invoke the divine through prayer, meditation, or ritual dance. Use symbols and objects that resonate with your spiritual path, fostering a profound connection with the transcendental energies.

Daily Elemental Practices

Infuse your daily life with the energies of the elements, creating a magical rhythm that aligns with the natural world. Small, intentional practices can become potent rituals that enhance your connection with earth, air, fire, water, and spirit.

Morning Grounding with Earth:

- Begin your day by standing barefoot on the earth. Feel the solid ground beneath you, connecting with the stability and grounding energy of the earth element. Express gratitude for the support the earth provides.

Mindful Breathing with Air:

- Throughout the day, engage in moments of mindful breathing. Pause and take several deep breaths, allowing the air element to clear your mind and invigorate your senses. Connect with the expansive nature of air.

Candle Meditation for Fire:

- In the evening, light a candle and focus on the flame. As you meditate, allow the energy of fire to spark inspiration within you. Visualize the flame illuminating your path and infusing you with courage.

Hydration Ritual with Water:

- Turn your daily hydration into a water-focused ritual. As you drink water, visualize it purifying and revitalizing your body. Connect with the flowing and adaptive energy of water.

Evening Reflection with Spirit:

- Before bedtime, engage in a moment of reflection or prayer to connect with the spiritual realm. Express gratitude for the day's experiences and seek guidance from the divine. Embrace the unity of spirit as you transition into the dream realm.

The Elemental Dance: An Integrated Approach

As a solitary witch, you have the flexibility to weave the energies of the elements seamlessly into your magical practice. Consider the following integrated approach, known as the Elemental Dance, which combines the qualities of each element into a harmonious and fluid ritual.

Elemental Dance Ritual

Preparation:

- Set up your sacred space with representations of each element—a candle for fire, incense for air, a bowl of water, soil or stones for earth, and a symbol of spirit.

Casting the Circle:

- Begin by facing each cardinal direction and invoking the corresponding element. As you turn, visualize the elemental energy enveloping you and forming a protective circle.

Earth Invocation:

- Stand facing north and connect with the energy of earth. Ground yourself, feel the stability beneath you, and express gratitude for the foundational support of the earth element.

Air Invocation:

- Turn to the east and connect with the energy of air. Inhale deeply, feeling the clarity and expansiveness of air. Express gratitude for the intellectual and communicative gifts of the air element.

Fire Invocation:

- Face south and connect with the energy of fire. Light a candle and focus on the flame. Feel the transformative and empowering energy of fire. Express gratitude for the passion and vitality it provides.

Water Invocation:

- Turn to the west and connect with the energy of water. Place your hands in a bowl of consecrated water or visualize the fluidity and healing energy of water. Express gratitude for the emotional and intuitive gifts of the water element.

Spirit Invocation:

- Stand in the center of your sacred space, facing upward. Connect with the energy of spirit, visualizing a radiant light above you. Express gratitude for the unity and transcendence of the spiritual realm.

Elemental Dance:

- Begin to move in a circular or spiraling pattern, incorporating dance, gestures, or symbolic movements that embody the qualities of each element. Feel the energies blending and flowing within you.

Unified Elemental Energy:

- As you dance, envision the elemental energies merging into a harmonious and balanced force within your being. Sense the interconnectedness of earth, air, fire, water, and spirit working together.

Gratitude and Closing:

- As you conclude the Elemental Dance, express gratitude for the energies of each element. Face each direction again, thanking the elemental forces for their presence. Close the circle, visualizing the protective energy dissipating.

Weaving Elemental Wisdom into Your Craft

Connecting with the elements and energies is a transformative journey that enriches your solitary witchcraft practice. The wisdom of earth, air, fire, water, and spirit becomes a guiding force, infusing your spells, rituals, and daily life with potent and harmonious energy. As you dance with the elements, embrace the profound interconnectedness of the natural world, and let the elemental energies weave a tapestry of magic in every facet of your solitary witchcraft journey. In the chapters ahead, we will delve deeper into the practical applications of elemental magic, providing you with spells, rituals, and insights to further enhance your craft.

Chapter Twelve

Understanding the Elemental Forces

In the enchanting realm of solitary witchcraft, the profound understanding of elemental forces forms the bedrock of magical wisdom. Each element—earth, air, fire, water, and spirit—holds a unique essence and energy that, when harnessed, empowers your spells, rituals, and daily life. This chapter delves into a deeper exploration of the elemental forces, unraveling the mysteries and unveiling the ways in which these potent energies shape and guide your solitary witchcraft journey.

Earth: The Grounding Anchor

As you journey through the landscape of elemental forces, Earth stands as the grounding anchor—the stabilizing force that connects you to the physical realm. This element encompasses the fertile soil beneath your feet, the sturdy rocks, and the ancient trees that whisper the wisdom of ages. Understanding the essence of Earth is vital for creating a solid foundation in your magical practice.

Qualities of Earth: Stability, fertility, nurturing.

Practical Applications: Grounding rituals, Green Witchcraft.

Connecting with Earth: Commune with nature, elemental symbols.

Air: The Breath of Inspiration

Air, the element of intellect and communication, dances through the skies, carrying the whispers of inspiration and the power of clear thought. Understanding the essence of Air opens pathways to intellectual clarity, effective communication, and the expansive realms of thought that fuel your magical pursuits.

Qualities of Air: Clarity, communication, inspiration.

Practical Applications: Breathwork, incense magic.

Connecting with Air: Wind observations, elemental symbols.

Fire: The Transformative Flame

Fire, a force of transformation and willpower, dances with passion and intensity. It is the element of creation and change, embodying the spark of life within every being. Understanding the essence of Fire ignites the flame of courage and empowers your magical workings.

Qualities of Fire: Transformation, willpower, passion.

Practical Applications: Candle magic, bonfire rituals.

Connecting with Fire: Candle meditation, elemental symbols.

Water: The Flow of Emotions and Intuition

Water, with its fluid and adaptable nature, symbolizes the ebb and flow of emotions and the depths of intuition. It is the source of purification and renewal, offering a gateway to the mysteries of the subconscious.

Understanding the essence of Water enhances your emotional intelligence and intuitive abilities.

Qualities of Water: Emotion, intuition, purification.

Practical Applications: Water scrying, ritual baths.

Connecting with Water: Moonlit reflections, elemental symbols.

Spirit: The Transcendent Unity

The fifth element, often referred to as spirit or ether, transcends the physical elements and embodies the essence of unity and interconnectedness. Understanding the essence of Spirit allows you to connect with the divine, your higher self, and the collective consciousness.

Qualities of Spirit: Unity, transcendence, divine connection.

Practical Applications: Meditation and contemplation, connection to higher self.

Connecting with Spirit: Dedication of sacred space, rituals of transcendence.

Harmonizing the Elemental Forces

Understanding the elemental forces is not merely an intellectual pursuit but an experiential journey that unfolds as you actively engage with each element. Harmonizing these forces within your magical practice involves recognizing their interconnectedness and weaving them together seamlessly. Consider the following insights to deepen your understanding and harmonize the elemental forces.

Interconnected Dance: Envision your magical practice as a dance with the elements. Allow Earth's stability to support Air's clarity, Fire's passion to fuel Water's intuition, and Spirit's transcendence to unite all elements in a harmonious dance.

Seasonal Alignment: Explore the seasonal correspondences of each element. Align your magical workings with the energy of the seasons, incorporating the qualities of Earth, Air, Fire, Water, and Spirit that are most potent during specific times of the year.

Elemental Attunement: Develop a deep attunement to each element by spending time in nature and observing its manifestations. Listen to the rustling leaves for Air, feel the warmth of the sun for Fire, touch the cool waters for Water, connect with the solidity of the earth beneath you, and sense the transcendent unity in the stillness of Spirit.

Magical Synergy: Create magical synergy by combining the energies of multiple elements in your rituals and spells. For example, infuse a grounding ritual with the purifying energy of Water or the inspirational qualities of Air.

The Elemental Tapestry of Your Craft

As a solitary witch, understanding the elemental forces is a key to unlocking the full potential of your magical practice. Earth, Air, Fire, Water, and Spirit weave a tapestry of energies that permeate every aspect of your journey. Embrace the essence of each element, dance with their forces, and let the elemental wisdom guide you on your solitary witchcraft path. In the chapters that follow, we will explore practical applications, spells, and rituals that harness the transformative power of the elemental forces, providing you with a rich tapestry of magical techniques to enhance your craft.

Chapter Thirteen

Grounding and Centering Techniques

In the intricate dance of solitary witchcraft, grounding and centering serve as foundational practices that connect you to the energies of the earth and your inner core. These techniques are essential for maintaining balance, focus, and stability in your magical endeavors. This chapter explores various grounding and centering techniques, providing you with a repertoire of practices to anchor your energy and enhance the potency of your solitary witchcraft.

The Importance of Grounding and Centering

Before delving into the techniques themselves, it's crucial to understand the significance of grounding and centering in the context of your magical practice.

Grounding: Grounding, also known as earthing, involves connecting with the energy of the earth to establish a stable foundation. Just as a tree roots itself in the soil to draw sustenance, grounding allows you to draw upon the earth's energies for stability, support, and a sense of rootedness. This practice is particularly vital when working with magical energies to ensure that excess energy is released into the earth, preventing energetic imbalances.

Centering: Centering involves finding your inner balance and aligning with your core essence. It is akin to locating your spiritual center of gravity—the point within yourself where you feel calm, focused, and in harmony with your intentions. Centering enables you to navigate the complexities of magical work with a clear mind and a steadfast sense of self.

Grounding Techniques

Earth Connection Meditation:

- Find a quiet and comfortable space where you won't be disturbed. Sit or lie down in a relaxed position.

- Close your eyes and take several deep breaths to calm your mind.

- Visualize roots extending from the soles of your feet, reaching deep into the earth.

- Feel the energy of the earth rising through these roots and into your body with each inhalation.

- Imagine any excess or stagnant energy flowing down through the roots and into the earth as you exhale.

- Continue this visualization until you feel a sense of connection, stability, and groundedness.

Grounding through Touch:

- Stand or sit comfortably with your feet flat on the ground.

- Focus on the sensation of your connection with the earth beneath you.

- Gently massage your hands together, creating warmth and energy.

- Place your hands on your heart or any part of your body that needs grounding.

- Feel the warmth and energy transferring from your hands, grounding and soothing the area.

Nature Walk Grounding:

- Take a leisurely walk in nature, whether it's a park, forest, or beach.

- Pay attention to each step, feeling the connection between your feet and the earth.

- Breathe in the natural scents, listen to the sounds around you, and absorb the colors and textures.

- Allow yourself to merge with the natural environment, grounding your energy in the beauty of the earth.

Centering Techniques

Breath-Centered Meditation:

- Sit comfortably with your spine straight and shoulders relaxed.

- Close your eyes and focus on your breath. Inhale deeply, feeling your lungs expand.

- Exhale slowly, releasing any tension or distractions.

- Continue this rhythmic breathing, allowing each breath to bring you into a centered and focused state.

- If your mind wanders, gently guide it back to the sensation of your breath.

Crystal Centering:

- Choose a crystal that resonates with you, such as clear quartz, amethyst, or selenite.

- Hold the crystal in your hands and close your eyes.

- Visualize a radiant light emanating from the crystal, enveloping you in a protective and centering energy.

- Feel the crystal's energy merging with your own, creating a harmonious balance within.

Elemental Centering:

- Find a quiet space and stand with your feet shoulder-width apart.

- Visualize the elements surrounding you—earth at your feet, air swirling around, fire igniting your spirit, water flowing through your emotions, and spirit connecting you to the divine.

- Envision these elemental energies converging at your center, creating a balanced and unified force within you.

- Feel the equilibrium of the elements aligning with your core essence.

Incorporating Grounding and Centering into Rituals

As a solitary witch, grounding and centering are invaluable tools that can enhance the effectiveness of your rituals and spellwork. Consider incorporating these practices into your magical endeavors to create a solid foundation and maintain a focused, balanced state.

Pre-Ritual Grounding

The pre-ritual phase holds a special significance in solitary witchcraft, acting as the gateway between the mundane and the magical realms. It is during this transitional period that you prepare your mind, body, and spirit to engage with the energies of the ritual. Grounding, as an integral part of pre-ritual practices, serves to establish a stable foundation, allowing you to approach the magical working with clarity, focus, and a deep connection to the earth's energies.

Cultivating Presence

Before delving into the intricate details of a ritual, take a few moments to cultivate presence. Sit or stand in a quiet space where you won't be disturbed. Close your eyes and begin by taking slow, deliberate breaths. As you breathe, let go of the concerns and distractions of the outside world. Visualize any mental chatter dissipating like mist, leaving behind a clear and tranquil mind.

This practice of cultivating presence is a form of grounding in itself, allowing you to shed the residue of daily life and step into the sacred space of your ritual with a focused and present mind. Feel the weight of your body against the earth, establishing a conscious connection with the physical realm.

Rooting into the Earth

An effective way to ground yourself in the pre-ritual phase is by connecting with the earth's energies. Whether you are indoors or outdoors, visualize roots extending from the soles of your feet, delving deep into the earth. Picture these roots intertwining with the rich soil, drawing up the earth's grounding energy.

As you engage in this visualization, allow any excess energy or tension to flow down these roots and into the earth. Feel the stabilizing force of the earth supporting you, anchoring your energy in preparation for the magical work ahead. This practice not only grounds you but also establishes a reciprocal flow of energy between yourself and the earth.

Sensory Grounding

Engaging your senses in the present moment is a powerful method of grounding before a ritual. Take a moment to observe and appreciate your surroundings. Feel the texture of objects around you, whether it's the cool surface of stones, the warmth of candlelight, or the softness of fabric.

Engage your sense of smell by taking in the scents of the ritual space. Whether it's the natural aroma of herbs, the sweet fragrance of incense, or the earthy smell of sacred oils, let these scents anchor you in the sensory experience of the present. Sensory grounding brings your awareness to the immediate environment, fostering a deeper connection to the ritual space.

Centering through Breath

Incorporate conscious breathwork as a means of centering and grounding before a ritual. Find a comfortable position and take slow, deliberate breaths. Inhale deeply, allowing the breath to fill your lungs, and exhale slowly, releasing any tension or preoccupations.

As you breathe, envision the breath as a conduit for energy, flowing through your body and creating a harmonious rhythm. With each inhalation, draw in the vital energies of the air. With each exhalation, release any stagnant or excess energy. This focused breathwork not only grounds you but also aligns your inner energies, preparing you for the sacred work ahead.

Intention Setting

Before officially commencing the ritual, take a moment for conscious intention setting. Reflect on the purpose and goals of the ritual, allowing your intentions to crystallize in your mind. This practice helps to align your energy with the specific magical workings you are about to undertake.

As you set your intentions, visualize them taking root within you, much like seeds planted in fertile soil. Feel the earth's energy supporting and nourishing these intentions, ensuring that they grow and manifest in alignment with your magical goals. This intentional grounding establishes a focused direction for your energy, enhancing the efficacy of your ritual work.

Ritual Preparation and Grounding

In addition to these specific grounding techniques, consider incorporating grounding into the overall ritual preparation. Whether you're consecrating tools, arranging altar items, or casting a protective circle, infuse each action with a mindful connection to the earth's energies. As you handle ritual objects, sense their connection to the physical world and the grounding influence they carry.

By weaving grounding practices into the pre-ritual phase, you set the stage for a magical working that is anchored, focused, and harmoniously connected to the energies of the earth. This intentional grounding becomes a ritual within itself, aligning your being with the sacred space you've created and paving the way for a transformative and potent magical experience.

Elemental Circle Casting

The circle is a symbol of unity, eternity, and the cyclical nature of existence. When casting a circle, witches create a sacred space that is neither fully in the mundane nor the magical realm. Elemental circle casting takes this a step further by calling upon the elemental energies to guard and bless the quarters of the circle.

Setting the Intention

Before beginning the casting process, set a clear intention for your ritual. Understand the purpose and goals you wish to achieve within the sacred space. Whether it's spellwork, divination, or communion with the divine, a well-defined intention guides the flow of energy within the circle.

Creating the Physical Circle

Start by physically marking the boundaries of your circle. This can be done with a wand, athame, or even by sprinkling salt or herbs along the circumference. As you move deosil (clockwise) to mark the circle, visualize a protective, shimmering barrier arising from the boundary.

Invoking the Elemental Quarters

Once the physical circle is established, turn your attention to the elemental quarters. Stand at the center of the circle facing east, the traditional starting point for calling the elements, and visualize the following as you invoke each element:

1. **East: Air**
   - **Visualization:** Picture gentle breezes, swirling clouds, and the expansive sky.

- **Invocation:** *"I call upon the element of Air, the breath of inspiration. May your clarity infuse this circle with intellect and communication. Hail and welcome!"*

2. South: Fire

- **Visualization:** Envision flickering flames, the warmth of the sun, and the transformative power of fire.

- **Invocation:** *"I call upon the element of Fire, the transformative flame. May your passion ignite this circle with courage and willpower. Hail and welcome!"*

3. West: Water

- **Visualization:** Imagine gentle waves, flowing rivers, and the cleansing power of water.

- **Invocation:** *"I call upon the element of Water, the flowing emotion. May your intuition cleanse this circle and bring the depths of the subconscious. Hail and welcome!"*

4. North: Earth

- **Visualization:** See solid rocks, fertile soil, and the stability of the earth.

- **Invocation:** *"I call upon the element of Earth, the grounding anchor. May your stability support this circle with abundance and manifestation. Hail and welcome!"*

Charging the Circle

After invoking each element, take a moment to feel the energies of the elements merging and harmonizing within the circle. Visualize the elemental forces standing guard at their respective quarters, forming a protective and empowering barrier around your sacred space.

Energy Alignment

Feel the energies of the elements aligning with your own energy, creating a symbiotic relationship. As the elements infuse the circle, sense the resonance of each element within your being.

Circumambulation

To further charge the circle, walk deosil around the perimeter, connecting with the energies of each quarter. With each step, sense the elemental energies amplifying and fortifying the protective barrier.

Working Within the Elemental Circle

Once the elemental circle is cast and charged, you are ready to commence your magical workings. Whether it's spellcasting, ritual observances, or divination, the elemental energies within the circle serve as both guardians and collaborators in your magical endeavors.

Post-Ritual Release

Just as you invoked the elemental energies to create the circle, releasing the circle involves bidding farewell to these energies with gratitude and respect. This acknowledgment ensures a harmonious relationship with the elemental forces and maintains a balanced exchange of energy.

Steps for Post-Ritual Release:

1. Thanking the Elemental Quarters:

Begin the post-ritual release by turning widdershins (counterclockwise) to face each elemental quarter, starting from the north. Express gratitude and thanks to each element, acknowledging their presence and the contributions they made to the ritual.

- **North:** *"I thank the element of Earth for grounding and stability. Hail and farewell!"*

- **West:** *"I thank the element of Water for intuition and cleansing. Hail and farewell!"*

- **South:** *"I thank the element of Fire for transformative passion. Hail and farewell!"*

- **East:** *"I thank the element of Air for inspiration and clarity. Hail and farewell!"*

2. Visualizing Elemental Dissolution:

As you bid farewell to each elemental quarter, visualize the energies dissipating back into their natural forms. Picture the earth returning to solid ground, water flowing freely, fire transforming into ambient warmth, and air dispersing into the atmosphere.

3. Circumambulation in Widdershins:

To further release the energies within the circle, walk widdershins around the perimeter. As you move, visualize the protective barrier of the circle gently dissolving, allowing the energies to return to their natural state. Sense the release of any residual energy that may linger within the circle.

4. Personal Grounding:

Once you have released the elemental quarters and walked widdershins around the circle, take a moment for personal grounding.

Stand at the center of the circle and visualize any excess or residual energy flowing down through your body and into the earth. Feel the stabilizing force of the earth supporting you.

5. Dispersal of Circle:

Finally, physically disperse the circle by either erasing the boundary with your hand, athame, or wand or by sweeping it away with a besom (broom). As you do this, envision the remnants of the circle returning to the natural elements from which it was drawn, leaving behind no trace of the magical boundary.

Weaving Stability and Focus into Your Craft

Grounding and centering are not isolated practices but woven threads that enhance the fabric of your solitary witchcraft journey. As you explore and integrate these techniques into your magical repertoire, you'll find yourself moving through the realms of energy with greater stability, focus, and a profound connection to the earth and your inner essence. In the chapters ahead, we will continue to delve into practical applications, spells, and rituals that complement and amplify the potency of grounding and centering in your solitary witchcraft practice.

Chapter Fourteen

Moon Magic and Lunar Phases

In the enchanting realm of solitary witchcraft, the moon holds a special place of prominence, weaving its ethereal threads through the tapestry of magical practices. As a solitary witch, attuning yourself to the lunar cycles and harnessing the magic of the moon opens doorways to profound insights, heightened intuition, and transformative spellwork. This chapter delves into the captivating world of moon magic, exploring the significance of lunar phases and offering insights on how to align your solitary witchcraft with the rhythmic dance of the moon.

The Lunar Tapestry: Understanding Moon Magic

- **Embodiment of Feminine Energy:** The moon, with its gentle glow and cyclical nature, is often seen as a symbol of the divine feminine. Embodying the energies of receptivity, intuition, and mystery, the moon provides a sacred mirror for the depths of the soul.

- **Reflecting Inner Realities:** Much like the moon reflects the light of the sun, it is believed to mirror the inner realities and emotions of those who gaze upon it. As a solitary witch, the moon becomes a powerful ally in exploring the hidden recesses of your psyche and tapping into your intuitive wisdom.

- **Cycles of Transformation:** The moon's ever-changing phases symbolize the cycles of life, death, and rebirth. Each lunar phase carries its unique energy, offering opportunities for manifestation, release, and inner reflection. Understanding these phases empowers you to synchronize your magical workings with the natural ebb and flow of cosmic energies.

The Eight Lunar Phases: Navigating the Celestial Rhythms

- **New Moon:** The new moon marks the beginning of the lunar cycle. It is a time of initiation, planting seeds of intention, and setting goals. In solitary witchcraft, the new moon is ideal for spells focused on new beginnings, personal growth, and fresh starts.

- **Waxing Crescent:** As the moon begins to wax, its crescent shape signifies growth and expansion. This phase is opportune for spells that involve building, attracting, and drawing energy. Harness the waxing crescent for endeavors related to manifestation and positive transformation.

- **First Quarter:** The first quarter, also known as the waxing half-moon, is a period of dynamic energy and action.

It's a time for overcoming obstacles, making decisions, and moving forward with projects. Solitary witches can utilize the first quarter for spells that involve strength, courage, and assertiveness.

- **Waxing Gibbous:** As the moon continues to wax, it enters the gibbous phase, signaling a time of refinement and fine-tuning. This phase is conducive to spellwork that involves polishing, enhancing, and honing skills. Solitary witches can utilize the waxing gibbous for endeavors related to self-improvement and mastery.

- **Full Moon:** The full moon, bathed in luminous splendor, is a potent time for maximum magical power. It is a climax of energy, making it ideal for spells related to manifestation, divination, and heightened psychic abilities. Solitary witches can bask in the full moon's brilliance to amplify the potency of their rituals.

- **Waning Gibbous:** Following the full moon, the waning gibbous phase encourages reflection, release, and letting go. It's a time to shed what no longer serves you and release any stagnant energy. Solitary witches can engage in spellwork that involves banishing, breaking habits, and decluttering during the waning gibbous.

- **Last Quarter:** The last quarter, also known as the waning half-moon, invites introspection and evaluation. It is a period for releasing negativity, resolving conflicts, and preparing for renewal. Solitary witches can engage in spellwork focused on banishing, clearing obstacles, and seeking closure during the last quarter.

- **Waning Crescent:** As the moon approaches the end of its cycle, the waning crescent phase signals a time for rest, recuperation, and introspection. It's a favorable period for solitude, dreamwork, and divination. Solitary witches can embrace the waning crescent for spells that involve rest, healing, and connecting with the inner self.

Lunar Magic Practices for Solitary Witches

- **Moon Bathing:** Engage in moon bathing during the full moon. Find a serene outdoor location, preferably where moonlight is unobstructed, and spend time basking in the moon's glow. Allow the lunar energies to cleanse and recharge your energy field.

- **Moon Water Ritual:** Harness the potent energy of the full moon to create moon water. Place a container of water under the full moon overnight, allowing it to absorb the lunar energies. Use the moon-charged water for rituals, spellwork, or as an energetic cleanser.

- **Divination under the Moon:** Practice divination during the waxing moon, especially on the night of the full moon. Whether using tarot cards, runes, or scrying tools, the heightened energy during this phase enhances the clarity of divinatory insights.

- **Charging Crystals:** Utilize the full moon's energy to charge and cleanse crystals. Place your crystals on a windowsill or in an outdoor space under the full moonlight. The lunar energy will infuse the crystals, enhancing their metaphysical properties.

- **New Moon Manifestation:** Harness the energy of the new moon for manifestation rituals. Set clear intentions, write them down, and perform a ritual to plant the seeds of your desires. As the moon waxes, visualize your intentions growing and coming to fruition.

- **Waning Moon Release:** During the waning moon, engage in rituals for release and letting go. Identify aspects of your life that no longer serve your highest good and perform ceremonies to release attachments, habits, or negative energy.

- **Dreamwork and the Waning Crescent:** Embrace the introspective energy of the waning crescent for dreamwork. Keep a dream journal and focus on dreams during this phase, seeking insights, guidance, and messages from the subconscious mind.

Creating Your Lunar Rituals: A Solitary Witch's Guide

- **Intention Setting:** Begin by setting clear intentions for your lunar rituals. Whether it's manifestation, release, or divination, clarity in your objectives enhances the potency of your magical workings.

- **Sacred Space Preparation:** Create a sacred space for your lunar rituals. This can be indoors or outdoors, but ensure it's a quiet and undisturbed environment where you can connect with the moon's energies.

- **Casting a Lunar Circle:** Consider casting a lunar-inspired circle for your rituals. Visualize the moon's radiant energy forming a protective boundary around your sacred space, amplifying the magical vibrations within.

- **Invocation of Lunar Energies:** Call upon the energy of the moon in your rituals. Invoke the lunar goddess or simply connect with the essence of the moon as a source of intuition, reflection, and magical power.

- **Moon Salutations:** Incorporate moon salutations into your rituals. These are simple gestures or movements that honor the moon and express gratitude for its influence on your magical workings.

- **Moonlit Spellwork:** Perform spellwork under the moonlight. Whether it's a full moon manifestation spell or a new moon release ritual, the lunar energies enhance the effectiveness of your magical intentions.

- **Moon Phases Correspondence:** Align your specific magical workings with the corresponding lunar phase. Match the nature of your spell or ritual with the energies associated with the current moon phase.

- **Reflection and Integration:** After completing your lunar rituals, take time for reflection. Journal your experiences, insights, and any messages received during the ritual. This reflective practice aids in the integration of the magical energies into your daily life.

Embracing the Lunar Mysteries

Moon magic, with its captivating allure and ancient mysteries, becomes a guiding beacon in the solitary witch's journey. By understanding the nuances of lunar phases and weaving them into your magical practices, you embark on a harmonious dance with the cosmic forces. Embrace the lunar mysteries, let the moonlight illuminate your path, and delve into the transformative power of solitary witchcraft under the enchanting glow of the moon. In the chapters that follow, we will continue our exploration of practical applications, spells, and rituals that deepen your connection to the mystical energies that surround and infuse your solitary witchcraft craft.

CHAPTER FIFTEEN

MOON SPELLS: HARNESSING LUNAR ENERGIES FOR MAGICAL WORKINGS

Moon spells are a powerful way for solitary witches to tap into the ever-shifting energies of the moon phases. These spells are crafted to align with specific lunar phases, maximizing the potency of your magical intentions. Whether you seek manifestation, release, or heightened intuition, these 12 moon spells provide a diverse range of magical workings for the solitary witch.

1. New Moon Prosperity Spell

Intent: Attracting Abundance and New Opportunities

Materials:

- Green candle

- Bay leaves

- Pen and paper

Procedure:

- Begin on the night of the new moon.

- Light the green candle, symbolizing prosperity.

- Write your financial goals on the paper.

- Fold the paper and place it under the candle.

- Burn bay leaves in the candle flame, visualizing your goals manifesting.

- Let the candle burn out completely.

2. Waxing Crescent Confidence Charm

Intent: Building Self-Confidence and Assertiveness

Materials:

- Moonstone crystal

- Chamomile tea

Procedure:

- Brew a cup of chamomile tea on the waxing crescent moon night.

- Hold the moonstone in your hands.

- Charge the tea by placing the moonstone in it.

- Drink the tea, absorbing the confidence-enhancing energies.

3. Full Moon Love Spell

Intent: Attracting Love and Positive Relationships

Materials:

- Pink or red candle

- Rose quartz crystal

- Vanilla essential oil

Procedure:

- Perform on the night of the full moon.

- Anoint the candle with vanilla oil.

- Place the rose quartz beside the candle.

- Light the candle, focusing on love and positive relationships.

- Let the candle burn while meditating on your desires.

4. Waxing Gibbous Career Boost

Intent: Advancing Career Goals and Ambitions

Materials:

- Yellow candle

- Citrine crystal

- Patchouli essential oil

Procedure:

- Initiate on the waxing gibbous moon.

- Anoint the candle with patchouli oil.

- Place the citrine crystal near the candle.

- Light the candle, envisioning career success.

- Allow the candle to burn out.

5. Full Moon Release Ritual

Intent: Letting Go of Negative Energy and Obstacles

Materials:

- Black candle

- Obsidian crystal

- Pen and paper

Procedure:

- Perform on the night of the full moon.

- Write negative aspects on the paper.

- Place the paper under the black candle.

- Light the candle, releasing negativity as it burns.

- Bury the ashes with gratitude for release.

6. Waning Gibbous Banishing Spell

Intent: Removing Unwanted Influences

Materials:

- White candle

- Clear quartz crystal

- Sage bundle

Procedure:

- Start on the waning gibbous moon night.

- Light the white candle for purity.

- Hold the clear quartz in your hands.

- Smudge the space with sage, banishing negativity.

- Extinguish the candle, sealing the banishing.

7. Last Quarter Forgiveness Ritual

Intent: Seeking Forgiveness and Healing

Materials:

- Blue candle

- Selenite crystal

- Lavender essential oil

Procedure:

- Initiate on the last quarter moon.

- Anoint the candle with lavender oil.

- Place the selenite crystal near the candle.

- Meditate on forgiveness as the candle burns.

- Allow the candle to extinguish naturally.

8. Waning Crescent Sleep Spell

Intent: Promoting Restful Sleep and Dreamwork

Materials:

- Lavender sachet

- Amethyst crystal

- Chamomile tea

Procedure:

- Begin on the waning crescent moon.

- Place the lavender sachet under your pillow.

- Hold the amethyst crystal before sleeping.

- Drink chamomile tea before bedtime.

- Focus on peaceful sleep and dream enhancement.

9. New Moon Cleansing Bath

Intent: Purifying and Releasing Energy

Materials:

- Epsom salt

- Rosemary essential oil

- White candle

Procedure:

- Prepare a bath on the new moon night.

- Add Epsom salt and a few drops of rosemary oil.

- Light a white candle for purity.

- Enter the bath, visualizing cleansing and release.

- Air-dry to let the energies disperse naturally.

10. Waxing Crescent Creativity Spell

Intent: Igniting Creative Inspiration and Ideas
Materials:

- Orange candle

- Carnelian crystal

- Cinnamon incense

Procedure:

- Begin on the waxing crescent moon.

- Light the orange candle for creativity.

- Hold the carnelian crystal, focusing on ideas.

- Burn cinnamon incense to stimulate creativity.

- Extinguish the candle when ready.

11. Full Moon Divination Ritual

Intent: Enhancing Psychic Abilities and Insight
  Materials:

- Purple candle

- Labradorite crystal

- Palo Santo for cleansing

Procedure:

- Perform on the night of the full moon.

- Cleanse the space with Palo Santo.

- Light the purple candle for spiritual insight.

- Hold the labradorite while practicing divination.

- Thank the energies and extinguish the candle.

12. Waning Gibbous Healing Spell

Intent: Physical and Emotional Healing
  Materials:

- Blue or green candle

- Aventurine crystal

- Lavender oil

Procedure:

- Begin on the waning gibbous moon.

- Anoint the candle with lavender oil.

- Place the aventurine crystal near the candle.

- Focus on healing energy as the candle burns.

- Allow the candle to extinguish naturally.

Remember to always practice ethical magic and respect the free will of others. Customize these spells to align with your specific intentions and feel the energies of the moon guide your solitary witchcraft journey.

Chapter Sixteen

Sun Magic and Seasonal Celebrations

In the vast tapestry of witchcraft, the sun stands as a radiant source of power, illuminating the path for solitary witches on their magical journey. As the wheel of the year turns, each season brings its unique energy, and harnessing the magic of the sun becomes a potent way for solitary practitioners to deepen their connection with the natural cycles. This chapter explores the realm of sun magic, guiding beginners through the significance of solar energies and the art of celebrating the changing seasons in solitary witchcraft.

The Essence of Sun Magic

The sun, a symbol of divine energy, is a wellspring of vitality and transformation. In solitary witchcraft, aligning with solar energies allows practitioners to tap into the life-giving force that sustains all living things. The sun represents not only physical warmth but also spiritual illumination and enlightenment.

Incorporating solar symbols into your magical practice deepens your connection with sun magic. Symbols like the sun wheel, solar cross, and depictions of the sun in various mythologies serve as conduits for channeling solar energy. As a solitary witch, you can create your unique symbols to personalize your practice.

Sun magic isn't confined to specific rituals or ceremonies; it can infuse your daily life. Begin your mornings by greeting the rising sun, acknowledging its life-giving energy. This simple act creates a daily connection with solar forces, fostering a harmonious relationship with the sun's transformative power.

Incorporate solar meditation into your practice to attune your energy with the sun. Find a quiet space outdoors during daylight hours, sit comfortably, and close your eyes. Visualize the sun's golden rays enveloping you, filling every cell with warmth and vitality. This meditation enhances your energetic alignment with solar forces.

Seasonal Celebrations in Solitary Witchcraft

Spring Equinox - Ostara: As the sun crosses the celestial equator, bringing balance between day and night, the Spring Equinox marks a time of renewal and growth. In solitary witchcraft, celebrate Ostara by decorating your altar with symbols of fertility, such as eggs and spring flowers. Perform rituals that focus on personal growth, new beginnings, and embracing the vitality of the returning sun. (Approximate Timing: March 20-23)

Beltane - Celebrating Solar Passion: Beltane, the May Day celebration, embraces the peak of spring and the burgeoning solar energy. In solitary witchcraft, kindle the Beltane bonfire to honor the sun's passionate force. Perform rituals that celebrate love, passion, and the union of the divine masculine and feminine energies. Dance around the fire, allowing the flames to ignite your inner fire. (Approximate Timing: April 30-May 1)

Summer Solstice - Litha: At the height of the sun's power, the Summer Solstice, or Litha, marks the longest day and shortest night of the year. In solitary witchcraft, honor the sun's zenith by crafting solar charms and talismans. Perform rituals that harness the sun's peak energy for personal empowerment, manifestation, and gratitude for the abundance of the season. (Approximate Timing: June 20-23)

Lammas - Harvesting Solar Abundance: As the first harvest festival, Lammas acknowledges the sun's role in ripening the fruits of the earth. In solitary witchcraft, create a Lammas altar adorned with grains, fruits, and symbols of the sun. Perform rituals that express gratitude for the solar abundance, harvest blessings, and contemplate the cycle of giving and receiving. (Approximate Timing: August 1)

Autumn Equinox - Mabon: Mabon, the Autumn Equinox, heralds the waning of solar energy and the onset of the darker half of the year. In solitary witchcraft, honor Mabon by creating a balance between light and shadow on your altar. Perform rituals that focus on introspection, balance, and expressing gratitude for the sun's sustaining energy throughout the growing season. (Approximate Timing: September 20-23)

Samhain - Embracing Solar Wisdom: As the veil between the worlds thins, Samhain invites solitary witches to tap into the wisdom of the departing sun. Create a Samhain altar adorned with solar symbols and items honoring departed ancestors. Perform rituals that seek guidance from the solar consciousness and honor the transformative power of the sun in the cycle of life and death. (Approximate Timing: October 31-November 1)

Winter Solstice - Yule: Yule, the Winter Solstice, marks the rebirth of the sun as the days begin to lengthen. In solitary witchcraft, celebrate Yule by decorating your altar with evergreens, candles, and symbols of the returning sun. Perform rituals that welcome the sun's rebirth, kindling the inner light within yourself and embracing the promise of longer days. (Approximate Timing: December 20-23)

Illuminating Your Solitary Path with Sun Magic

Sun magic and seasonal celebrations provide solitary witches with a profound way to attune themselves to the natural rhythms of the earth and cosmos. By embracing the transformative power of the sun and honoring the changing seasons, practitioners of solitary witchcraft embark on a journey of self-discovery, empowerment, and spiritual growth. As you delve into the realms of sun magic, let the radiant energy of the sun illuminate your solitary path, guiding you through the cycles of life, death, and rebirth. In the chapters that follow, we will continue our exploration of practical applications, spells, and rituals that deepen your connection to the mystical energies that surround and infuse your solitary witchcraft craft.

Chapter Seventeen

Embracing Solar Energies

In the tapestry of magical practices, embracing solar energies opens a gateway to profound transformation and empowerment. As a solitary witch, weaving the radiant essence of the sun into your craft not only connects you with the vibrant energies of the cosmos but also empowers your journey of self-discovery. This chapter delves into the art of embracing solar energies, guiding beginners through rituals, spells, and techniques to infuse their solitary witchcraft practice with the illuminating power of the sun.

Understanding Solar Energies

At the heart of our solar system, the sun serves as a cosmic dynamo, radiating energy that sustains life on Earth. In solitary witchcraft, recognizing the sun as a symbol of divine power allows you to tap into its life-giving force. This celestial body embodies not only physical warmth but also spiritual enlightenment, making it a potent ally in your magical pursuits.

Solar symbols, rich with archetypal significance, resonate deeply in the realms of magic. The sun wheel, representing the cyclical nature of life, and various sun gods and goddesses from different mythologies serve as conduits for solar energies. As a solitary witch, exploring and incorporating these symbols into your craft enhances your connection with the transformative power of the sun.

Solar energies bring forth the alchemy of light and shadow, symbolizing the interplay between the conscious and subconscious mind. Embracing solar energies invites you to explore both aspects of yourself, acknowledging the brilliance of your strengths and the shadows that hold hidden wisdom. Through this alchemical process, you can achieve balance and self-realization in your magical practice.

Practical Techniques for Embracing Solar Energies

1. Solar Meditation: Begin your journey of embracing solar energies with a simple yet powerful solar meditation. Find a quiet space outdoors during daylight hours. Sit comfortably, close your eyes, and turn your face towards the sun. Visualize the golden rays enveloping you, permeating every cell with warmth and vitality. As you bask in this solar embrace, allow the energy to infuse you with a sense of empowerment and clarity.

2. Sunlit Spellwork: Take advantage of natural sunlight in your spellwork. Whenever possible, perform your magical rituals outdoors during sunrise or sunset. Feel the sun's energy amplifying your intentions and charging your spells with its transformative power. The direct communion with the sun's energy enhances the efficacy of your solitary witchcraft practice.

3. Solar Charging Ritual: Create a solar charging ritual to infuse your magical tools with the energy of the sun. Place your tools, such as crystals, athame, or charms, on a clean surface outdoors under the sunlight. As you do, express your intention for these tools to absorb the solar energies. Visualize the items glowing with a radiant light, charged and ready for your magical workings.

4. Solar Affirmations: Craft solar affirmations that resonate with your personal intentions. Speak these affirmations during your solar meditation or as part of your daily practice. Affirmations such as "I am a beacon of solar empowerment" or "I embrace the transformative light within" align your mindset with the radiant energies of the sun.

5. Solar Talismans and Charms: Create solar talismans or charms to carry with you throughout the day. Choose symbols that represent the sun or incorporate solar gemstones like citrine or sunstone. Infuse these objects with your intentions for personal empowerment, courage, and enlightenment. As you carry them, feel the solar energies surrounding and protecting you.

Solar Rituals for Self-Empowerment

1. Solar Empowerment Ritual: Perform a solar empowerment ritual during a sunny day. Find a secluded outdoor spot and sit or stand, facing the sun. Close your eyes, raise your arms, and visualize golden light pouring down from the sun, filling your entire being. As you breathe deeply, affirm your intentions for personal empowerment and transformation.

2. Solar Cleansing Bath: Create a solar cleansing bath to purify and rejuvenate your energy. Fill your bathtub with warm water and add solar-associated herbs like chamomile or calendula. As you soak, visualize the water absorbing solar energies, cleansing away any negativity or stagnant energy. Feel the revitalizing power of the sun embracing you.

3. Solar Invocation for Clarity: Craft a solar invocation ritual to seek clarity and insight. Begin by creating a sacred space outdoors.

Light a yellow candle to represent the sun and invoke solar deities or energies that resonate with you. As you meditate, ask for clarity in your thoughts and decisions. Feel the sun illuminating your mind, bringing a sense of mental clarity and understanding.

4. Solar Blessing for Personal Growth: Perform a solar blessing ritual to invoke the sun's energy for personal growth. Choose a sunny morning or afternoon to conduct the ritual outdoors. Use symbols of growth, such as potted plants or seeds. As you bless these symbols under the sun, express gratitude for the opportunities for personal growth and transformation that the solar energies bring.

Integrating Solar Energies Into Daily Life

Solar Greeting Ritual: Incorporate a solar greeting into your daily routine. As you wake up each morning, take a moment to acknowledge the rising sun. Stand near a window or step outside, close your eyes, and greet the sun with gratitude. This simple act establishes a daily connection with solar energies, infusing your day with positivity and vitality.

Solar-Inspired Creativity: Engage in creative activities inspired by solar energies. Paint or draw representations of the sun, crafting your personal symbols for empowerment and enlightenment. Use solar-inspired colors like gold and yellow in your artistic endeavors to amplify the connection with the transformative power of the sun.

Sunlit Reflection Journal: Maintain a sunlit reflection journal to record your experiences, thoughts, and insights gained through embracing solar energies. Take a few moments each day to jot down your reflections on how the sun's energy has influenced your mindset, actions, or magical practice. This reflective journaling deepens your awareness of the transformative journey you undertake as a solitary witch.

Sun Affirmations: Harnessing the Radiant Energies

- **Solar Empowerment Spell:** *Intent:* To enhance personal empowerment and vitality. *Spell:* Stand in a sunny spot, arms raised. Visualize golden light enveloping you. Affirm, *"I am empowered by the sun's radiant energy,"* feeling the solar warmth infusing every part of your being.

- **Sunrise Renewal Spell:** *Intent:* To start the day with positivity and rejuvenation. *Spell:* Face the sunrise, and visualize its golden rays filling you with renewed energy. Speak words of gratitude for the new day and visualize any negativity dissolving in the sun's light.

- **Solar Clarity Meditation:** *Intent:* To gain mental clarity and insight. *Spell:* Sit facing the rising or setting sun. Breathe deeply, envisioning the sun dissolving mental fog. Affirm, *"I embrace the clarity of the sun's wisdom,"* letting the solar illumination clear your thoughts.

- **Sunlit Confidence Charm:** *Intent:* To boost confidence and courage. *Spell:* Carry a charm adorned with solar symbols. Hold it in the sunlight, affirming, *"Like the sun, I shine with confidence."* Visualize the charm glowing with solar energy, infusing you with courage.

- **Solar Creativity Spell:** *Intent:* To inspire creative expression. *Spell:* During a sunny day, engage in a creative activity.

Paint or draw solar symbols, using gold and yellow colors. As you create, let the sun's energy flow into your artistic expressions.

- **Sunstone Energy Infusion:** *Intent:* To charge a sunstone for energy and vitality. *Spell:* Place a sunstone in sunlight. Visualize the stone absorbing solar energy. Hold it, affirming, *"I carry the sun's vitality within."* Use the charged sunstone for increased energy throughout the day.

- **Solar Blessing for Abundance:** *Intent:* To attract abundance and prosperity. *Spell:* Choose a sunny morning. On your altar, place symbols of abundance. Thank the sun for its life-giving energy, affirming, *"As the sun provides, so does abundance flow into my life."*

- **Solar Healing Ritual:** *Intent:* To harness the sun's healing energy. *Spell:* Sit in sunlight, visualize the sun's rays penetrating any discomfort. Affirm, *"I am healed by the sun's transformative touch,"* feeling the warmth bringing healing energy.

- **Solar Harmony Spell:** *Intent:* To bring balance and harmony. *Spell:* During a solar noon, create a mandala with symbols of balance. As you meditate on it, affirm, *"In the sun's light, I find balance,"* absorbing the harmonizing energies.

Radiant Empowerment on Your Solitary Path

Embracing solar energies in your solitary witchcraft practice opens doors to radiant empowerment, self-discovery, and spiritual growth.

As you infuse your magical journey with the transformative power of the sun, remember that the essence of solar energies resides within you. Through solar meditation, practical techniques, and empowering rituals, you align with the cosmic dynamo that fuels your magical path.

As you continue to explore the luminous realms of solitary witchcraft, let the radiant energies of the sun guide you through the alchemy of light and shadow. Your solitary path is illuminated by the brilliance of your inner sun, a source of infinite power waiting to be awakened. May the solar energies empower your craft, enlighten your spirit, and lead you toward the radiant fulfillment of your magical aspirations. In the chapters that follow, we will delve deeper into advanced practices, uncovering the mysteries that further enrich your solitary witchcraft journey.

Chapter Eighteen

Herbal Magic and Plant Correspondences

In the enchanted world of solitary witchcraft, the use of herbs transcends the boundaries of the mundane, offering a tapestry of magical possibilities. Herbal magic, a practice deeply rooted in ancient traditions, connects the solitary witch to the subtle energies residing within the plant kingdom. From the delicate petals of a flower to the sturdy roots of a tree, each herb holds unique correspondences, making it a potent ally in the craft. In this chapter, we will embark on a journey through the verdant realms of herbal magic, exploring plant correspondences, magical applications, and the art of creating sacred herbal blends.

The Essence of Herbal Magic

Herbal magic is a sacred communion with the wisdom of nature. As a solitary witch, working with herbs allows you to tap into the vibrational energies that plants possess. Each herb vibrates with its unique frequency, carrying the signature of its elemental, planetary, and magical correspondences. By attuning yourself to these energies, you become a co-creator in the dance of natural forces.

Plants speak a language older than words, a silent dialogue that transcends the limitations of human communication. Through their leaves, flowers, and roots, plants convey messages of healing, transformation, and magic. In solitary witchcraft, learning to decipher the language of plants opens portals to hidden realms, unveiling the mysteries of the green world.

Herbs engage the senses, captivating with their fragrances and flavors. The aromatic oils, resins, and compounds within herbs possess therapeutic and magical properties. In herbal magic, the alchemy of fragrance and flavor becomes a potent medium for crafting spells, charms, and potions. The sensory experience of working with herbs enhances the potency of your magical workings.

Plant Correspondences and Elemental Alignments

Earth: Earthly herbs, rooted in the soil, align with the element of earth. Plants such as patchouli, vetiver, and comfrey draw upon the stabilizing and grounding energies of the earth element. In solitary witchcraft, earth-aligned herbs are employed for spells related to stability, prosperity, and physical well-being.

Air: Herbs that carry a delicate fragrance and are associated with the airy realms align with the element of air. Lavender, rosemary, and mint embody the airy energies, lending themselves to spells focused on intellect, communication, and mental clarity. Use air-aligned herbs in rituals that involve thought, communication, and the realm of ideas.

Fire: Plants associated with the sun's warmth and vitality align with the fiery element. Cinnamon, basil, and ginger harness the fiery energies, making them ideal for spells related to passion, courage, and transformative magic. Incorporate fire-aligned herbs when working with spells that require intensity, energy, and ignition.

Water: Herbs that thrive near water sources or have soothing, watery properties align with the element of water. Chamomile, jasmine, and yarrow carry the gentle, flowing energies of water, making them suitable for spells related to emotions, intuition, and healing. Include water-aligned herbs in rituals that involve emotional well-being and psychic work.

Magical Applications of Herbs

Herbal Correspondences in Spellwork: In solitary witchcraft, the art of herbal magic lies in understanding the correspondences of each herb and aligning them with your magical intent. Select herbs that resonate with the energy of your spell, enhancing its potency. For example, if crafting a spell for protection, consider herbs like rosemary, bay, or angelica, each known for their protective qualities.

Herbal Charms and Talismans: Infuse herbs into charms and talismans to create potent magical tools. Select herbs based on their correspondences to amplify the energy of the charm. Carry a sachet filled with protective herbs for personal safety or create a talisman using herbs associated with love and attraction. The physical presence of herbs in charms establishes a tangible link between the magical and mundane realms.

Herbal Infusions and Elixirs: Crafting herbal infusions and elixirs is a sacred way to ingest the magical properties of herbs. Create teas, tinctures, or infused waters using herbs aligned with your intent. Drink herbal infusions to attune your energies to the magical properties of the herbs, promoting well-being, clarity, or spiritual connection.

Herbal Baths and Cleansing Rituals: Herbal baths offer a luxurious and magical way to cleanse and purify. Select herbs with correspondences that align with your cleansing intent. Rosemary, lavender, and eucalyptus, for example, are ideal choices for a purification bath. As you immerse yourself in the herbal waters, visualize the cleansing energies of the herbs washing away any negativity or stagnant energies.

Herbal Anointing and Oil Blends: Anointing with herbal oils is a time-honored practice in solitary witchcraft. Infuse oils with herbs aligned with your magical goals, creating a magical potion that can be applied to candles, tools, or yourself. Use oils for anointing in rituals, spells, or meditation, allowing the aromatic and magical properties of the herbs to envelop you.

Creating Sacred Herbal Blends

Intuition as a Guide: The creation of sacred herbal blends is an intuitive process, guided by your magical intent and connection to the energies of the plants. Allow your intuition to be the compass as you select herbs for a blend. Trust your instincts and attune to the vibrations of the herbs, sensing how they harmonize with each other.

Correspondences in Harmony: When crafting herbal blends, consider the correspondences of each herb to ensure harmony within the blend. If your intent is to create a blend for love and harmony, choose herbs associated with love, such as rose, jasmine, and hibiscus. Aligning the correspondences of the herbs enhances the overall magical efficacy of the blend.

Timing and Lunar Influences: The timing of herbal magic aligns with the phases of the moon and planetary influences. Consider the lunar phase that corresponds to your magical intent when creating herbal blends. For example, crafting a blend for abundance may be most potent during the waxing moon, while a blend for releasing and letting go may be crafted during the waning moon.

Ritual of Blending: The act of blending herbs is a sacred ritual in itself. As you mix the herbs, infuse them with your intent, and visualize the magical energy of each herb intertwining. Use tools like a mortar and pestle to grind the herbs, further infusing them with your energy. The rhythmic motion of blending becomes a dance, harmonizing the energies of the herbs into a cohesive whole.

The Green Grimoire of Solitary Witchcraft

Herbal magic, the green grimoire of solitary witchcraft, invites you to explore the realms of plant wisdom, energy, and correspondence. Through the language of plants, you connect with the elemental forces, aligning your magical intent with the vibrant energies residing within the green world. As you venture further into the herbal realms, may the spirits of the plants be your guides, unveiling the secrets of their fragrant and magical tapestry.

In the chapters that follow, we will delve into advanced practices, uncovering the mysteries of the craft, and further enriching your solitary witchcraft journey. May your herbal blends be potent, your magical garden thrive, and the green magic of the earth weave its enchantment into your solitary path.

CHAPTER NINETEEN

EXPLORING MAGICAL PROPERTIES OF HERBS

In the sacred tapestry of solitary witchcraft, the exploration of the magical properties of herbs unfolds as a mystical journey into the heart of nature's mysteries. As a solitary witch, delving into the hidden realms of herbcraft allows you to unlock the potent energies, correspondences, and alchemical secrets concealed within the green foliage. In this chapter, we will embark on a voyage of discovery, unraveling the magical properties of herbs, understanding their unique signatures, and learning how to harness their energies in your solitary magical practice.

The Alchemy of Herbal Magic

At the heart of herbal magic lies the alchemical dance of synergy and correspondences. Each herb possesses a unique vibrational frequency, a magical signature that resonates with specific intentions, elements, planets, and energies. Exploring the magical properties of herbs involves understanding the subtle interplay between their correspondences, aligning them with your magical goals, and tapping into the ancient wisdom embedded within the green allies.

Building an intuitive connection with herbs is a cornerstone of solitary witchcraft. Allow your senses to become attuned to the energies emanating from each herb. Touch the leaves, inhale the fragrance, and feel the vibrational resonance within your being. As you cultivate an intuitive bond with herbs, you become a conduit for their magical properties, opening channels of communication between the plant kingdom and your magical practice.

When exploring the magical properties of herbs, your intent becomes the guiding force. Clearly define your magical goals and visualize the desired outcome as you work with herbs. Visualization enhances the potency of herbal magic, allowing you to infuse your intent into the plant energies. As you embark on magical workings with herbs, envision the desired manifestation, and feel the energies of the herbs aligning with your purpose.

Herbs of Protection and Warding

Rosemary (Rosmarinus officinalis): A guardian of the sacred realms, rosemary is renowned for its protective properties. In solitary witchcraft, this herb is often used to create charms, sachets, and herbal bundles for safeguarding spaces. Hang a bundle of dried rosemary near entrances to your home or ritual space to create a barrier against negative energies. The aromatic essence of rosemary serves as a potent ward, dispelling unwanted influences and establishing a protective shield.

Mugwort (Artemisia vulgaris): Mugwort, with its silvery leaves and ethereal presence, is a powerful ally in protective magic. It is associated with the moon and dreams, making it ideal for enhancing psychic protection. In solitary witchcraft, mugwort can be incorporated into dream pillows or sachets placed under your pillow to ward off nightmares and unwanted spiritual intrusions. Burn dried mugwort during ritual cleansings to purify and protect your magical space.

Black Salt: While not a single herb, black salt is a magical concoction crafted from ingredients such as salt, ashes, and charcoal. In solitary witchcraft, black salt is employed for its potent protective qualities. Sprinkle it around the perimeter of your home or ritual space to create a protective boundary. You can also incorporate black salt into spellwork or rituals to banish negative energies and entities.

Herbs of Love and Attraction

Rose (Rosa spp.): The timeless symbol of love, the rose, holds unparalleled magical properties in the realm of love and attraction. In solitary witchcraft, use dried rose petals to create love sachets, charms, or bath blends. Place a single red rose on your altar to invoke the energies of love and passion. Incorporate rose petals into love spells or rituals to enhance romantic connections and attract loving relationships.

Jasmine (Jasminum spp.): With its intoxicating fragrance, jasmine is associated with love, sensuality, and attraction. In solitary witchcraft, jasmine can be utilized in love spells, charms, and ritual baths to invoke the energies of passion and romance. Anoint candles with jasmine oil during love-focused rituals, allowing the aromatic essence to infuse the sacred space with alluring energies.

Damiana (Turnera diffusa): Damiana, a magical herb with aphrodisiac properties, is renowned for its association with love and passion. In solitary witchcraft, damiana can be used in spellwork, charm bags, or herbal blends designed to enhance sensuality and attract love. Incorporate damiana into rituals focused on self-love and empowerment, embracing the energies of passion and desire.

Herbs of Healing and Well-being

Lavender (Lavandula spp.): Lavender, with its calming and soothing properties, is a versatile herb in solitary witchcraft, especially in rituals of healing and well-being. Create sachets filled with dried lavender to promote relaxation and restful sleep. Burn lavender as an incense during rituals focused on emotional healing and stress reduction. Incorporate lavender into herbal baths or oils to cleanse and rejuvenate the mind, body, and spirit.

Chamomile (Matricaria chamomilla): Chamomile, with its gentle and nurturing essence, is associated with healing and relaxation. In solitary witchcraft, chamomile can be used in spells, charms, and rituals aimed at soothing emotional distress and promoting overall well-being. Drink chamomile tea before meditation or divination to enhance your connection with the subtle energies of the plant and foster a sense of inner peace.

Echinacea (Echinacea purpurea): Revered for its immune-boosting properties, echinacea is a magical herb of protection and healing. In solitary witchcraft, echinacea can be incorporated into rituals or charms designed to strengthen the immune system and ward off illness. Use echinacea in herbal blends or tinctures to harness its protective energies, creating a shield against physical and energetic maladies.

Herbs of Divination and Psychic Enhancement

Mugwort (Artemisia vulgaris): Beyond its protective qualities, mugwort is esteemed for its connection to divination and psychic enhancement. In solitary witchcraft, mugwort can be burned as incense during divination sessions to heighten intuitive insights and strengthen psychic abilities. Carry a small sachet of dried mugwort during divination practices or place it under your pillow to enhance dreamwork and spiritual attunement.

Bay Laurel (Laurus nobilis): Bay laurel, with its rich history and association with wisdom, is a powerful herb for divination. In solitary witchcraft, use bay leaves in rituals, charms, or spells focused on enhancing intuitive abilities and gaining insight. Write divinatory questions on bay leaves and burn them during divination sessions, allowing the fragrant smoke to carry your inquiries to the spiritual realms.

Frankincense (Boswellia spp.): Revered for its sacred and purifying properties, frankincense is a versatile herb in enhancing psychic abilities. Burn frankincense resin as incense during meditation or divination to create a conducive atmosphere for spiritual insights. Incorporate frankincense into ritual oils or blends to amplify your connection with the higher realms and facilitate communication with spiritual guides.

Crafting Herbal Talismans and Amulets

Intent-infused Talismans: Craft talismans using herbs aligned with your magical intent. Select herbs based on their correspondences and magical properties, incorporating them into a small pouch or charm bag. Carry the talisman with you to attract the desired energies or protect against specific influences. The physical presence of herbs within the talisman serves as a conduit for the magical intent.

Empowering Amulets: Amulets, infused with the energies of specific herbs, become powerful symbols of protection and empowerment. Choose herbs that align with the purpose of the amulet, whether it's for love, prosperity, or spiritual attunement. Anoint the amulet with herbal oils, consecrating it in alignment with your magical intent. Wear the amulet as a sacred charm, allowing the herbal energies to surround you.

Ritual Charging: Charge talismans and amulets in ritual space to infuse them with heightened magical energy. During a ritual, place the talisman or amulet on your altar, surrounded by candles, crystals, and other correspondences aligned with your intent. Visualize the energies of the herbs intertwining with the magical forces present in the ritual space, empowering the talisman with the desired magical properties.

A Herbal Grimoire Unveiled

Exploring the magical properties of herbs in solitary witchcraft is an intimate dance with the forces of nature, a journey that unveils the hidden wisdom of the green realms. As you infuse your practice with the energies of protective, loving, healing, and divinatory herbs, may the subtle vibrations of the plant kingdom become the sacred ink in the pages of your herbal grimoire.

In the chapters that follow, we will delve into advanced practices, unraveling the mysteries of the craft, and further enriching your solitary witchcraft journey. May your herbal magic flourish, your spellwork be potent, and the whispers of the green allies guide you along your solitary path.

CHAPTER TWENTY

HERBAL SPELLS AND BREWS: A MAGICAL TAPESTRY OF NATURE'S BOUNTY

Embark on a journey through the realms of herbal magic with these 12 enchanting spells and brews. Harness the potent energies of nature's bounty, but tread with caution. Be mindful of potential allergies to ensure your magical experience remains safe and delightful.

Warning: Before engaging in any herbal magic, be aware of potential allergies. Perform a patch test before using herbs on the skin or consuming them. If you have known allergies to specific herbs, seek alternatives or consult with a medical professional. Always ensure the safety of yourself and others in your magical practices.

1. Spell for Protection

Ingredients:

- Rosemary (protection)

- Basil (warding off negativity)

- Black salt (banishing)

Spellwork: Combine rosemary, basil, and black salt in a small sachet. Hold it in your hands, focusing on your intent for protection. Hang the sachet near entrances to create a protective barrier.

2. Love Attraction Brew

Ingredients:

- Rose petals (love)

- Jasmine flowers (attraction)

- Honey (sweetening)

Brewing: Steep rose petals and jasmine flowers in hot water. Add a spoonful of honey, stirring clockwise. Drink the brew before performing love spells or seeking romantic connections.

3. Healing Charm

Ingredients:

- Lavender (healing)

- Chamomile (soothing)

- Clear quartz crystal (amplification)

Charm Crafting: Bundle lavender and chamomile, tying them with a string. Attach a clear quartz crystal to enhance the healing energies. Carry the charm for physical and emotional well-being.

4. Psychic Enhancement Incense

Ingredients:

- Mugwort (psychic abilities)

- Bay leaves (divination)

- Frankincense resin (spiritual insight)

Incense Crafting: Grind dried mugwort, bay leaves, and frankincense resin. Burn the mixture during divination or meditation to enhance psychic awareness.

5. Prosperity Sachet

Ingredients:

- Patchouli (prosperity)

- Cinnamon (wealth)

- Green aventurine crystal (abundance)

Sachet Creation: Blend patchouli and cinnamon in a small sachet. Add a green aventurine crystal for financial luck. Keep the sachet in your wallet or on your altar.

6. Moon Magic Bath

Ingredients:

- Jasmine petals (lunar energy)

- Moonstone crystal (intuition)

- Epsom salt (cleansing)

Bath Ritual: Add jasmine petals and a moonstone crystal to your bath along with Epsom salt. Soak in the magical energies to enhance intuition and dreamwork.

7. Banishing Brew

Ingredients:

- Black cohosh (banishing)

- Salt (purification)

- Dragon's blood resin (protection)

Brewing: Boil black cohosh, salt, and dragon's blood resin in water. Strain and use the brew to cleanse and banish negativity from your space.

8. Prosperity Oil Infusion

Ingredients:

- Basil leaves (wealth)

- Cinnamon sticks (success)

- Carrier oil (almond, jojoba)

Infusion Ritual: Place basil leaves and cinnamon sticks in a jar. Cover with carrier oil and let it sit in sunlight for a lunar cycle. Strain and use the infused oil in prosperity spells.

9. Grounding Spell

Ingredients:

- Patchouli (grounding)

- Cedarwood (stability)

- Hematite crystal (grounding)

Spellwork: Blend patchouli and cedarwood essential oils. Anoint a hematite crystal with the blend and carry it to stay grounded and centered.

10. Divination Tea

Ingredients:

- Mugwort (divination)

- Yarrow (psychic awareness)

- Peppermint (clarity)

Tea Brewing: Steep mugwort, yarrow, and peppermint in hot water. Drink the tea before divination sessions for heightened psychic insights.

11. Self-Confidence Sachet

Ingredients:

- Sunflower petals (confidence)

- Orange peel (positivity)

- Citrine crystal (empowerment)

Sachet Creation: Mix sunflower petals and orange peel in a sachet. Add a citrine crystal to amplify self-confidence energies. Carry it for a boost of empowerment.

12. Spiritual Purification Bath

Ingredients:

- Sage leaves (spiritual purification)

- Eucalyptus leaves (cleansing)

- Amethyst crystal (spiritual connection)

Bath Ritual: Combine sage leaves and eucalyptus leaves in your bathwater. Add an amethyst crystal for spiritual purification and connection.

Chapter Twenty-One

Crystal Magic and Stone Energies

In the sacred realm of solitary witchcraft, the potent energies of crystals and stones unveil themselves as ancient allies, offering a kaleidoscope of magical possibilities. As a solitary witch, delving into the mysteries of crystal magic becomes a journey of connection with the Earth's profound energies and a dance with the vibrational frequencies embedded within the mineral kingdom. In this chapter, we will explore the enchanting world of crystal magic, uncover the unique energies of various stones, and learn how to harness their powers in solitary magical practice.

The Living Earth: Crystals as Magical Allies

Crystals and stones are not mere inanimate objects; they are imbued with the living essence of the Earth. Formed over eons through geological processes, each crystal carries the energetic imprints of the Earth's evolution. As a solitary witch, working with crystals allows you to tap into this vibrational resonance, connecting with the ancient wisdom stored within the crystalline structures.

Crystals are elemental allies, each resonating with specific elemental forces. Earth, air, fire, and water are encapsulated within the crystalline lattice, offering a diverse array of energies for magical workings. Understanding the elemental correspondences of crystals enhances your ability to attune their energies with your intent, creating a harmonious synergy between the elemental forces and your magical goals.

In solitary witchcraft, envisioning the Earth as a vast, interconnected web of crystal energy can deepen your connection with the magical energies of stones. Just as a spider weaves its web, crystals form a metaphysical lattice that interconnects with the energies of the Earth and the cosmos. This web becomes a tapestry through which you can weave your magical intentions, attuning to the subtle currents of energy that flow through the crystal matrix.

Selecting and Connecting with Crystals

Choosing crystals for your magical work often begins with intuition. Allow yourself to be drawn to a particular crystal, trusting the subtle currents of energy that guide your selection. As a solitary witch, the intuitive connection with crystals becomes a sacred dialogue, where the energies of the stones resonate with the energies within your being.

Just as individuals resonate with different frequencies, so do crystals. Explore various crystals and pay attention to how each one makes you feel. The personal resonance between you and a crystal is a key factor in successful magical workings. Listen to the whispers of the stones, for they may reveal profound insights about your magical journey.

Before incorporating crystals into your magical practice, it's essential to cleanse and charge them. Crystals have the ability to absorb and store energy, and cleansing ensures that they are free from any previous influences. Methods such as smudging with sage, bathing in moonlight, or placing them on a bed of salt can cleanse the stones. Charging is the process of infusing the crystals with your intent, aligning their energies with your magical goals.

Exploring the Energetic Landscape of Crystals

Quartz Varieties: Quartz crystals, with their myriad varieties, are versatile allies in solitary witchcraft. Clear quartz serves as a powerful amplifier, enhancing the energies of other crystals. Rose quartz resonates with the energy of love and compassion, making it ideal for heart-centered magic. Smoky quartz grounds and dispels negative energies, while amethyst enhances spiritual insight. Delve into the quartz family to discover the unique energies each variety brings to your magical practice.

Protective Stones: Crystals such as black tourmaline, obsidian, and hematite are stalwart guardians in the realm of protection magic. Black tourmaline forms a protective shield against negativity, obsidian acts as a psychic cleanser, and hematite grounds and shields the aura. Incorporate these stones in charms, amulets, or rituals to create potent protective barriers around yourself and your sacred space.

Creativity and Inspiration: When seeking to ignite the flames of creativity and inspiration, turn to crystals like carnelian, citrine, and orange calcite. Carnelian stimulates creative expression, citrine brings abundance and joy, and orange calcite invigorates the creative flow. Carry or place these crystals in your creative space to infuse it with vibrant and uplifting energies.

Healing Energies: Amethyst, rose quartz, and clear quartz are renowned for their healing properties. Amethyst soothes the mind and promotes spiritual growth, rose quartz fosters emotional healing and self-love, and clear quartz amplifies overall healing energies. Utilize these crystals in rituals, meditations, or crystal grids to facilitate physical, emotional, and spiritual well-being.

Spiritual Insight and Intuition: For those on a quest for spiritual insight and enhanced intuition, crystals such as lapis lazuli, moonstone, and labradorite become invaluable allies. Lapis lazuli opens the third eye and enhances psychic abilities, moonstone connects with lunar energies, and labradorite unveils hidden truths. Work with these stones to deepen your spiritual practice and attune to intuitive guidance.

Crystal Magic in Rituals and Spellwork

Crystal Grids: Creating crystal grids is a potent form of crystal magic, where stones are arranged in a geometric pattern to amplify their energies. As a solitary witch, design crystal grids based on your magical intent. Whether it's for manifestation, healing, or protection, the geometric arrangement of crystals forms a sacred energy matrix that radiates your magical intent into the cosmos.

Amulets and Talismans: Infuse the energies of specific crystals into amulets or talismans to carry their magical properties with you. Choose stones aligned with your intent and create a wearable charm. Wear the amulet to enhance your personal power, protection, or to attract specific energies into your life.

Crystal Elixirs: Harness the vibrational energies of crystals through elixirs. Place crystals in water, allowing their energies to infuse the liquid. Use the crystal-infused water in rituals, spellwork, or as a personal elixir to attune to the magical properties of the stones. Ensure that the crystals used are safe for making elixirs, as some crystals may contain toxic elements.

Scrying and Divination: Crystals, with their reflective and translucent qualities, become powerful tools for scrying and divination. Use crystal balls, polished stones, or crystal wands as scrying tools to peer into the depths of the magical realms. The energies of the crystals enhance intuitive insights, making them conduits for receiving divinatory messages.

Creating Your Crystal Grimoire

Personal Crystal Journal: As a solitary witch, documenting your experiences with crystals in a personal crystal journal becomes a sacred practice. Record the energies, correspondences, and insights gained from each crystal. Include details such as the date of acquisition, cleansing methods, and the magical workings in which the crystals were employed. Your crystal grimoire becomes a treasure trove of wisdom, offering guidance and inspiration for future magical endeavors.

Energetic Alignments: Explore the energetic alignments between crystals and other magical correspondences. Note the elemental, planetary, and zodiacal associations of each crystal. This comprehensive understanding allows you to weave intricate spells, rituals, and magical workings that align with the cosmic currents flowing through the crystal kingdom.

Personal Experiences: Share your personal experiences and synchronicities with crystals in your journal. Document dreams, visions, or intuitive messages received during meditation with crystals. Your personal anecdotes become a rich tapestry of your evolving relationship with the magical energies of the stones.

Crystal Whispers in Solitude

In the solitary witch's journey, the whispers of crystals become an intimate conversation with the Earth's heartbeat. As you weave the energies of stones into your magical practice, may the crystal whispers guide you through the mysteries of the craft, deepening your connection with the living essence of the Earth. In the chapters that follow, we will delve into advanced practices, unraveling the hidden threads of the craft, and further enriching your solitary witchcraft journey. May the crystal magic you cultivate illuminate your path with radiant energies and unveil the hidden wonders of the magical realms.

CHAPTER TWENTY-TWO

CHOOSING AND CLEANSING CRYSTALS

In the mystical realm of solitary witchcraft, the selection and preparation of crystals stand as a pivotal gateway to the potent energies woven into the fabric of the Earth. As a solitary witch, the process of choosing and cleansing crystals is not merely a mundane task but a sacred communion with the living essence of the mineral kingdom. This chapter serves as your guide, unraveling the art of intuitive crystal selection and the essential steps involved in purifying these magical allies.

Intuitive Selection: Trusting Your Inner Guide

The journey into crystal magic often commences with an intuitive pull toward a particular stone. As a solitary witch, you are urged to trust this inner guide, the subtle whispers of your own being that draw you toward specific crystals. It's a dance of energies, an unspoken dialogue between your essence and that of the crystals.

Begin by exploring a variety of crystals, allowing yourself to be drawn to them without preconceived notions. Hold each stone in your hands, feeling its energy, and pay attention to any sensations, emotions, or insights that arise. The crystals that resonate with your unique energetic signature are likely to be the ones aligned with your magical intent.

Personal Resonance: A Sacred Dialogue

Each individual resonates with different frequencies, and this principle extends to crystals. In solitary witchcraft, the process of choosing crystals is an intimate journey of forging a personal resonance with these Earth treasures. Pay attention to how each crystal makes you feel—physically, emotionally, and spiritually.

For instance, holding a piece of rose quartz may evoke feelings of warmth, love, and compassion, while an amethyst may bring a sense of tranquility and spiritual insight. Your personal resonance with a crystal goes beyond intellectual understanding; it is a subtle yet profound connection that forms the basis of a sacred dialogue between you and the crystal kingdom.

Cleansing and Charging: Honoring the Sacred Exchange

Before delving into the magical workings with crystals, it is imperative to cleanse and charge them. Crystals, being energetic sponges, absorb energies from their surroundings. Cleansing serves to remove any residual influences from the crystal, returning it to its pure and untainted state. Charging, on the other hand, aligns the crystal with your specific magical intent, creating a harmonious resonance between the stone and your purpose.

Cleansing Methods:

- **Smudging:** Pass the crystals through the smoke of sacred herbs such as sage, palo santo, or cedar. Allow the cleansing smoke to envelop the crystals, purifying them on an energetic level.

- **Moonlight Bath:** Place the crystals under the light of the full moon, allowing the lunar energies to cleanse and recharge them. This method is particularly potent for stones associated with intuition and emotions.

- **Sunlight Charge:** Some crystals benefit from a bath in the energizing rays of the sun. However, exercise caution, as prolonged exposure can fade the colors of certain stones. Limit sun charging to brief intervals or use this method for stones like citrine that thrive in sunlight.

- **Earth Connection:** Burying crystals in the Earth for a period allows them to reconnect with the grounding energies of the Earth. This method is especially effective for stones associated with grounding and stability.

- **Sound Cleansing:** Immerse your crystals in the purifying vibrations of sound. You can use singing bowls, tuning forks, or even your voice to create resonant sounds that cleanse and clear the energetic field of the crystals.

Charging Rituals:

- **Intent Meditation:** Hold the crystal in your hands, focus on your magical intent, and visualize energy flowing from your being into the crystal. See the stone radiating with the specific vibrations aligned with your purpose.

- **Elemental Charging:** Place your crystals on or near natural elements during your charging ritual. For instance, align crystals associated with water with a flowing stream or place earth-associated stones on soil or sand. This elemental infusion enhances their magical potency.

- **Visualization:** Envision a stream of radiant light descending from the cosmos, flowing through your being, and transferring into the crystal. This visualization not only charges the crystal but also creates a deeper connection between you and the stone.

Navigating the Diverse World of Crystals

As a solitary witch, exploring the diverse world of crystals opens up a vast array of magical possibilities. Each crystal possesses unique energies and correspondences, making them valuable allies for specific magical intents. Here are insights into a few crystal families and their magical attributes:

1. Quartz Varieties: Quartz, with its myriad variations, serves as a versatile foundation in crystal magic. Clear quartz acts as a potent amplifier, enhancing the energies of other crystals. Rose quartz resonates with love and compassion, while smoky quartz provides grounding and dispels negativity.

2. Protective Stones: Black tourmaline, obsidian, and hematite stand as guardians in protection magic. Black tourmaline shields against negativity, obsidian cleanses psychic energies, and hematite grounds and protects the aura.

3. Creativity and Inspiration: Carnelian, citrine, and orange calcite are catalysts for creativity and inspiration. Carnelian stimulates creative expression, citrine attracts abundance, and orange calcite invigorates the creative flow.

4. Healing Energies: Amethyst, rose quartz, and clear quartz are renowned for their healing properties. Amethyst soothes the mind, rose quartz fosters emotional healing, and clear quartz amplifies overall healing energies.

5. Spiritual Insight and Intuition: Lapis lazuli, moonstone, and labradorite serve as allies for spiritual insight. Lapis lazuli enhances psychic abilities, moonstone connects with lunar energies, and labradorite unveils hidden truths.

Integration into Rituals and Spellwork

With your chosen and cleansed crystals in hand, you can now integrate them into your solitary witchcraft rituals and spellwork. Here are a few ways to incorporate crystals into your magical practice:

1. Crystal Grids: Craft intricate crystal grids based on your magical intent. These geometric arrangements amplify the energies of the stones, creating a potent energy matrix radiating your magical goals into the cosmos.

2. Amulets and Talismans: Infuse the energies of specific crystals into wearable amulets or talismans. This allows you to carry the magical properties of the crystals with you, serving as constant reminders and sources of empowerment.

3. Crystal Elixirs: Harness the vibrational energies of crystals through elixirs. Place crystals in water and allow their energies to infuse the liquid. Use the crystal-infused water in rituals, spellwork, or as a personal elixir to attune to the magical properties of the stones.

4. Scrying and Divination: Utilize crystals with reflective and translucent qualities, such as crystal balls, polished stones, or crystal wands, as powerful tools for scrying and divination. The energies of the crystals enhance intuitive insights, making them conduits for receiving divinatory messages.

Creating Your Personal Crystal Grimoire

As a solitary witch, documenting your experiences with crystals in a personal crystal grimoire becomes a sacred practice. Record the energies, correspondences, and insights gained from each crystal. Include details such as the date of acquisition, cleansing methods, and the magical workings in which the crystals were employed. Your crystal grimoire becomes a treasure trove of wisdom,

Honoring the Crystal Allies

Choosing and cleansing crystals is not a mere ritual; it is a sacred dance with the living essence of the Earth. As a solitary witch, your connection with crystals goes beyond the physical realm—it is a communion of energies, a silent dialogue with ancient wisdom. In the chapters that follow, we will delve deeper into advanced practices, unveiling the hidden threads of crystal magic and enriching your solitary witchcraft journey. May your chosen crystals guide you, protect you, and amplify the radiant energies of your solitary path.

Chapter Twenty-Three

Crystal Spellwork

Spell 1: Amplifying Intuition

Best Time: Perform during the waxing moon phase, especially on Thursdays, known for enhancing intuition and spiritual growth.

Intent: Enhance intuitive abilities.

Procedure: Choose a quiet and serene space for meditation. Place the amethyst on your forehead and the lapis lazuli just above it. Close your eyes, take deep breaths, and focus on opening your third eye. Let the energy flow through you. Repeat the spell during the meditation.

Affirmation: *"With amethyst's insight and lapis lazuli's wisdom, my intuition unfolds. As these crystals align, intuition sharpens, ancient wisdom awakens. So mote it be."*

Spell 2: Abundance Attraction

Best Time: Perform during the waxing moon on a Thursday, associated with Jupiter, the planet of abundance.

Intent: Attract abundance and prosperity.

Procedure: Sit in a comfortable position with the citrine and green aventurine in your hands. Visualize a golden light surrounding you and permeating your aura. Repeat the spell with confidence and belief in the abundance you're attracting.

Affirmation: *"Citrine's glow, Aventurine's flow, abundance comes, let it grow. As I will, so mote it be."*

Spell 3: Emotional Healing Bath

Best Time: Conduct this spell during the full moon, especially on Mondays, linked to emotional energies.

Intent: Emotional healing and release.

Procedure: Add rose quartz and moonstone to a warm bath. As you soak, visualize the crystals infusing the water with healing energies. Relax and let go of emotional burdens. Recite the spell with sincerity.

Affirmation: *"Water and stone, heal and release, emotions flow, inner peace increase. In the waters' embrace, I find healing grace. So mote it be."*

Spell 4: Protection Ward

Best Time: Perform during the waning moon phase for banishing negativity, particularly on Saturdays, a day associated with protection.

Intent: Create a protective barrier.

Procedure: Place black tourmaline and smoky quartz at the corners of your home or around your sacred space. Envision a protective barrier forming. Repeat the spell as you focus on the stones' protective energies.

Affirmation: *"Stones of night, stones of might, protect this space day and night. As I will, so mote it be."*

Spell 5: Creativity Boost

Best Time: Conduct this spell during the waxing moon, especially on Wednesdays, associated with communication and creativity.

Intent: Ignite creativity.

Procedure: Hold carnelian and orange calcite while engaging in a creative activity. Visualize a flame of inspiration igniting within you. Recite the spell as you immerse yourself in the creative process.

Affirmation: *"Stones of fire, inspire desire, creativity flows, as my talent glows. By the flame's embrace, my creativity I now chase. So mote it be."*

Spell 6: Healing Energy Infusion

Best Time: Perform this spell during the full moon or when needed for healing, on Sundays, associated with healing energies.

Intent: Infuse healing energies.

Procedure: Place clear quartz and amethyst on your heart chakra. Visualize a gentle stream of healing energy flowing through your body. Recite the spell, focusing on the stones' healing properties.

Affirmation: *"Quartz so clear, Amethyst dear, healing energies appear. By the crystal's might, I am healed and whole tonight. So mote it be."*

Spell 7: Psychic Shield

Best Time: Perform during the waxing moon or on Mondays for heightened psychic abilities.

Intent: Strengthen psychic protection.

Procedure: Hold labradorite and black obsidian. Envision a shimmering shield of iridescent light surrounding you. Repeat the spell, feeling the psychic shield becoming impenetrable.

Affirmation: *"Labradorite's gleam, obsidian's dream, psychic shield, powerful and supreme. By the stones' embrace, protection in every space. So mote it be."*

Spell 8: Communication Clarity

Best Time: Conduct this spell during the waxing moon, especially on Wednesdays, known for enhancing communication.

Intent: Enhance communication skills.

Procedure: Carry blue lace agate and sodalite with you during important conversations. Visualize clear communication and understanding. Repeat the spell before engaging in any dialogue.

Affirmation: *"Stones of blue, words true, communication flows through and through. By the stones' grace, clarity in every case. So mote it be."*

Spell 9: Love Magnetism

Best Time: Perform during the waxing moon or on Fridays, associated with love and relationships.

Intent: Attract love and positive relationships.

Procedure: Place rose quartz and rhodonite in your bedroom. Visualize an atmosphere of love and harmony. Repeat the spell, focusing on attracting positive and loving relationships.

Affirmation: *"Love's embrace, in every space, harmonious bonds, true love's chance. By the stones' power, love blooms like a flower. So mote it be."*

Spell 10: Dreamweaver's Delight

Best Time: Conduct this spell during the waxing or full moon, especially on Mondays, known for enhancing dreamwork.

Intent: Enhance dream recall and lucidity.

Procedure: Place amethyst and moonstone under your pillow before sleep. Visualize vivid dreams and heightened awareness. Repeat the spell to experience lucid dreams.

Affirmation: *"Dreamweaver's grace, crystals embrace, lucidity and recall, in sleep enthrall. By the stones' might, dreams come alive in the night. So mote it be."*

Spell 11: Confidence Charm

Best Time: Perform during the waxing moon or on Sundays, associated with personal power and confidence.

Intent: Boost self-confidence.

Procedure: Carry sunstone and tiger's eye with you during situations requiring confidence. Visualize a golden aura of self-assurance. Repeat the spell, feeling your confidence soar.

Affirmation: *"Stones of fire, boost desire, confidence rise, like the sun in the skies. By the stones' might, confidence takes flight. So mote it be."*

Spell 12: Release and Renewal

Best Time: Perform during the waning moon, especially on Saturdays, associated with banishing and renewal.

Intent: Release negative energy and invite renewal.

Procedure: Hold smoky quartz and clear quartz. Visualize old, stagnant energy leaving and making room for renewal. Repeat the spell, feeling a sense of release and revitalization.

Affirmation: *"Smoke's embrace, clear and pure grace, release the old, let the new unfold. By the stones' power, I am renewed every hour. So mote it be."*

Chapter Twenty-Four

Crystal Elixirs

Tranquil Harmony Elixir

Intent: Promote inner calm and balance.

Crystals: Amethyst, Aquamarine

Procedure: Cleanse the crystals and place them in a glass jar. Fill the jar with spring water and let it sit in moonlight overnight. In the morning, drink the elixir to promote tranquility and inner harmony.

Affirmation: *"As I sip this elixir pure, tranquility within will endure."*

Vitality Boost Elixir

Intent: Enhance energy and vitality.

Crystals: Carnelian, Citrine

Procedure: Cleanse the crystals and place them in a glass jar. Fill the jar with spring water and let it sit in sunlight for a day. Drink the elixir in the morning to boost energy and vitality.

Affirmation: *"With each sip, vitality grows, energy within me overflows."*

Heart Healing Elixir

Intent: Promote emotional healing and love.

Crystals: Rose Quartz, Rhodonite

Procedure: Cleanse the crystals and place them in a glass jar. Fill the jar with spring water and let it sit in sunlight for a day. Drink the elixir to open the heart and facilitate emotional healing.

Affirmation: *"As I drink, my heart's embrace, healing love in every trace."*

Clear Vision Elixir

Intent: Enhance clarity and insight.

Crystals: Clear Quartz, Selenite

Procedure: Cleanse the crystals and place them in a glass jar. Fill the jar with spring water and let it sit in moonlight overnight. Drink the elixir in the morning to gain clarity and insight.

Affirmation: *"Crystal clear, vision near, insight guides without a fear."*

Grounding Earth Elixir

Intent: Connect with grounding energies.

Crystals: Hematite, Smoky Quartz

Procedure: Cleanse the crystals and place them in a glass jar. Fill the jar with spring water and let it sit in the earth for a day. Drink the elixir to enhance grounding and stability.

Affirmation: *"Rooted deep, like ancient trees, grounding flows with each sip, it frees."*

Intuitive Flow Elixir

Intent: Enhance intuition and psychic abilities.

Crystals: Labradorite, Moonstone

Procedure: Cleanse the crystals and place them in a glass jar. Fill the jar with spring water and let it sit in moonlight overnight. Drink the elixir to open your intuitive channels.

Affirmation: *"As I drink this mystic blend, intuition rises, like a friend."*

Solar Power Elixir

Intent: Boost confidence and personal power.

Crystals: Sunstone, Tiger's Eye

Procedure: Cleanse the crystals and place them in a glass jar. Fill the jar with spring water and let it sit in sunlight for a day. Drink the elixir to ignite your personal power.

Affirmation: *"Solar might, within me ignite, confidence rises, like a kite."*

Serenity Sleep Elixir

Intent: Promote calm and restful sleep.

Crystals: Lepidolite, Howlite

Procedure: Cleanse the crystals and place them in a glass jar. Fill the jar with spring water and let it sit by your bedside for a night. Drink the elixir before sleep for a tranquil night.

Affirmation: *"Sip by sip, as I lay, serenity comes, in dreams I sway."*

Creative Spark Elixir

Intent: Ignite creativity and inspiration.

Crystals: Orange Calcite, Sodalite

Procedure: Cleanse the crystals and place them in a glass jar. Fill the jar with spring water and let it sit in sunlight for a day. Drink the elixir to fuel your creative spark.

Affirmation: *"Creativity, like a flame, ignites within, with every sip's claim."*

Stress Relief Elixir

Intent: Alleviate stress and tension.

Crystals: Blue Lace Agate, Lepidolite

Procedure: Cleanse the crystals and place them in a glass jar. Fill the jar with spring water and let it sit in moonlight overnight. Drink the elixir to release stress and bring peace.

Affirmation: *"With each drop, stress departs, tranquility flows, soothing hearts."*

Prosperity Flow Elixir

Intent: Attract abundance and prosperity.

Crystals: Green Aventurine, Citrine

Procedure: Cleanse the crystals and place them in a glass jar. Fill the jar with spring water and let it sit in sunlight for a day. Drink the elixir to invite prosperity into your life.

Affirmation: *"Prosperity flows, with every sip it grows."*

Self-Love Radiance Elixir

Intent: Enhance self-love and acceptance.

Crystals: Rose Quartz, Rhodonite

Procedure: Cleanse the crystals and place them in a glass jar. Fill the jar with spring water and let it sit in moonlight overnight. Drink the elixir to foster self-love and acceptance.

Affirmation: *"In every sip, love I find, for myself, gentle and kind."*

Chapter Twenty-Five

Divination for Solitary Witches

In the vast realm of witchcraft, divination stands as a mystical tool, offering insights and understanding through the interpretation of signs, symbols, or tools. For solitary witches, free from group dynamics, divination provides a personal and intimate connection to the unseen forces, aiding in navigating the magical journey. In this chapter, we explore various divination methods suitable for solitary witchcraft, delving into the mystical realms where intuition meets ancient wisdom.

Exploring Divination Practices

Divination Defined:

Divination is the practice of seeking knowledge through the interpretation of signs, symbols, or tools. Solitary witches can choose from various divination practices that align seamlessly with their craft.

1. Tarot Reading:

Tarot cards, with their visual language transcending time, provide a powerful tool for self-readings and personal introspection.

2. Runes:

Ancient symbols on stones or wood, runes offer a grounded and primal form of divination.

3. Crystal Scrying:

Using crystal balls, black mirrors, or polished crystals, scrying opens a portal to the subconscious mind.

4. Pendulum Divination:

The pendulum, responding to energy, becomes a tool for direct communication with intuition.

5. Numerology:

Numbers, with their universal language, offer insights into the magical journey through calculations and associations.

Incorporating Divination into Solitary Rituals

Creating a Divination Ritual:

Designing rituals that align with personal energy and preferences allows solitary witches to incorporate divination effectively.

Sacred Space Preparation:

Create a sacred space with candles, incense, or meaningful objects to enter a focused state.

Grounding and Centering:

Connect with the earth's energy, visualize roots, and draw up stabilizing energy.

Setting Intentions:

Clearly state intentions for the divination session to channel focus.

Choosing Divination Tools:

Select tools such as tarot cards, runes, crystals, or a pendulum based on intuition.

Quiet Reflection:

Take moments for quiet reflection, clearing the mind and attuning to subtle energies.

Asking Questions:

Pose specific, open-ended questions to receive nuanced and insightful responses.

Interpretation:

Trust intuition in interpreting symbols, patterns, or images that emerge during divination.

Expressing Gratitude:

Conclude the ritual by expressing gratitude for the guidance received, strengthening the bond with divine energies.

Closing Thoughts on Divination:

As a solitary witch, divination becomes a bridge between the ancient and the contemporary. Embrace the city's rhythm, explore its symbols, and infuse your practice with the vibrant energy of urban life. Through the art of divination, solitary witches unlock the mysteries that lie beneath the surface, gaining profound insights into their magical journey. Divination becomes a guide, a companion, and a source of profound wisdom for the solitary witch.

Chapter Twenty-Six

Tarot, Runes, and Other Divination Tools

In the tapestry of solitary witchcraft, the art of divination weaves intricate patterns, offering insights and guidance into the mystical realms. As a solitary witch, the selection of divination tools becomes a deeply personal and empowering journey. In this chapter, we explore the rich world of divination, focusing on three prominent tools: Tarot cards, Runes, and an array of other divination tools that resonate with the solitary practitioner.

Tarot Cards: Unlocking the Mysteries

Tarot cards, with their roots stretching into the mists of time, are a treasure trove of symbolism and archetypes. The traditional Tarot deck consists of 78 cards, divided into the Major and Minor Arcana. Each card carries its own unique energy, offering a visual language that speaks to the subconscious mind.

The Major Arcana, comprised of 22 cards, represents significant life events and spiritual lessons. From The Fool's journey of beginnings to The World's culmination of cycles, these cards delve into profound aspects of the human experience.

The 56 cards of the Minor Arcana delve into everyday aspects of life, with four suits representing the elements—Wands (Fire), Cups (Water), Swords (Air), and Pentacles (Earth). Each suit unfolds a narrative, mirroring the challenges and triumphs encountered on the solitary witch's path.

For the solitary witch, Tarot cards serve as a mirror reflecting the energies surrounding their magical journey. The process of reading Tarot involves drawing cards and interpreting their symbolism in the context of a specific question or situation. Trusting intuition and allowing the cards to tell a story enhances the depth and accuracy of the reading.

In solitary practice, creating personalized Tarot rituals enhances the connection between the witch and the cards. Rituals may involve cleansing the deck, charging the cards with intention, or dedicating a specific space for Tarot readings. Establishing a sacred bond with the cards deepens the insights gained during readings.

Runes: Ancient Wisdom in Symbolic Stones

Runes, ancient symbols rooted in Nordic and Germanic traditions, encapsulate primal energies and wisdom. Traditionally carved onto stones or wooden pieces, each Rune carries a distinct meaning and connection to natural forces. The 24 symbols in the runic alphabet, known as the Elder Futhark, hold profound insights into the mysteries of existence.

Solitary witches can craft their own set of Runes using stones, wood, or other materials. Carving or painting the symbols onto the chosen medium imbues the Runes with personal energy. This act of creation establishes a bond between the witch and the ancient wisdom encapsulated in the symbols.

The practice of Rune casting involves drawing the symbols and interpreting their positions and relationships. The placement of the Runes and their interactions reveal insights into the past, present, and future. As the solitary witch casts the Runes onto a cloth or directly onto the earth, they enter into a sacred dialogue with the forces that guide their magical journey.

In solitary witchcraft, integrating Runes into rituals amplifies their magical significance. Whether inscribing Runes onto candles, incorporating them into spellwork, or using them as a focal point during meditation, these symbols become allies, enhancing the witch's connection to the energies of the natural world.

Other Divination Tools: Expanding the Toolkit

Crystal Scrying:

The mystical art of scrying involves gazing into a reflective surface to receive intuitive insights. Crystals, with their unique energies, serve as potent tools for scrying. Whether using a crystal ball, a black mirror, or any polished crystal surface, the solitary witch can attune to the subtle messages and symbols that emerge during scrying sessions.

Pendulum Divination:

A pendulum, suspended from a chain or cord, responds to the energy surrounding a question or situation. In pendulum divination, the solitary witch holds the pendulum over a surface or chart and observes its movements to receive answers. This simple yet powerful tool becomes a direct link to intuition and the unseen forces at play.

Numerology:

Numbers, with their universal language, offer a unique perspective on the magical journey. Solitary witches can explore numerology by calculating life path numbers, exploring the significance of specific dates, or analyzing numerical patterns in their surroundings. Numerology becomes a divination tool when applied to guide decision-making and deepen self-discovery.

Crafting Personalized Divination Practices

While Tarot cards, Runes, crystals, pendulums, and numerology offer structured approaches to divination, the solitary witch may feel drawn to other tools intuitively. Shells, feathers, mirrors, or any object with personal significance can become a divination tool when infused with intention and used with focused intent.

Incorporating divination into sacred space deepens the connection between the witch and the mystical energies at play. Whether using candles, incense, or sacred objects, the creation of a sacred atmosphere enhances the receptivity of the divination session.

In the solitary practice of witchcraft, intuition becomes a trusted guide. As the solitary witch engages with divination tools, trusting intuitive impressions and interpretations enriches the divination experience. The tools serve as conduits for the witch's innate wisdom to surface and guide their magical journey.

A Tapestry of Insight

In the realm of solitary witchcraft, Tarot cards, Runes, and other divination tools unfold a tapestry of insight and guidance. As the solitary witch delves into the symbolism, energies, and wisdom encapsulated in these tools, they embark on a journey of self-discovery and magical exploration. Whether casting Runes, drawing Tarot cards, or gazing into a crystal, the art of divination becomes a sacred dialogue between the witch and the unseen forces that shape their solitary path.

Chapter Twenty-Seven

Developing Your Intuition

In the tapestry of solitary witchcraft, intuition emerges as a guiding force, a silent ally that whispers insights and nudges the practitioner along the path of magical discovery. This chapter delves into the profound realm of intuition, exploring its nature, nurturing its growth, and understanding its role in the solitary witch's journey.

Intuition, often referred to as the "sixth sense," is a form of inner knowing that transcends logic and rationality. It's a subtle language spoken by the soul, a connection to the unseen forces that weave through the fabric of existence. In the realm of solitary witchcraft, developing and trusting one's intuition becomes a cornerstone of magical practice.

The first step in developing intuition is cultivating awareness. Solitary witches, attuned to the ebb and flow of energies, learn to listen to the whispers of their inner selves. This heightened awareness involves paying attention to subtle cues, gut feelings, and the sensations that arise in response to different situations.

Nature, with its rhythmic cycles and primal energies, serves as a powerful ally in nurturing intuition. Solitary witches often find that spending time in natural settings enhances their intuitive abilities. Whether it's a walk in the woods, sitting by a flowing stream, or observing the dance of flames in a bonfire, nature becomes a sacred teacher, imparting its wisdom to those who attune to its frequencies.

Meditation and Stillness

The practice of meditation becomes a gateway to the depths of intuition. Solitary witches engage in regular meditation sessions, creating moments of stillness where the mind can quieten, and the intuitive voice can rise. Through meditation, witches learn to navigate the realms beyond the conscious mind, tapping into the wellspring of intuitive insights.

Dreamwork and Symbolism

Dreams, the ethereal landscapes of the subconscious, offer a rich tapestry of symbols and messages. Solitary witches pay close attention to their dreams, recognizing them as a realm where intuition freely communicates. Keeping a dream journal, deciphering symbols, and exploring the emotions associated with dreams enhance the witch's ability to decode the language of intuition.

Understanding Energy

In the solitary practice of witchcraft, sensitivity to energy becomes a cornerstone of intuitive development. Witches learn to perceive the subtle currents of energy that flow through all things. By understanding the nuances of energy, witches can discern the vibrations and frequencies that carry intuitive messages.

Trusting Inner Promptings

Intuition often speaks through inner promptings—those gentle nudges or strong feelings that guide decision-making. Solitary witches learn to trust these inner promptings, recognizing that the intuitive voice holds insights beyond the grasp of the logical mind. Trust becomes a bridge between the seen and the unseen, allowing intuition to unfold.

Rituals for Intuitive Development

Solitary witches weave rituals into their practice to specifically enhance intuitive abilities. These rituals may involve calling upon deities or spirit guides associated with intuition, crafting personalized spells to open the channels of inner knowing, or engaging in divination practices that deepen the connection to intuitive insights.

Creating an Intuitive Space

In the realm of solitary witchcraft, creating a sacred and intuitive space is crucial. Whether it's an altar adorned with symbols that resonate with intuition, a dedicated meditation corner, or a natural setting that becomes a sanctuary, the space itself becomes a conduit for intuitive energies to flow freely.

Working with Divination Tools

Divination tools, such as Tarot cards, Runes, or scrying crystals, become allies in the development of intuition. Solitary witches engage with these tools not merely as instruments of prophecy but as mirrors reflecting the intuitive currents within. Through regular practice with divination, witches sharpen their intuitive faculties, learning to interpret symbols and messages with increasing clarity.

Embracing Synchronicities:

Synchronicities, those meaningful coincidences that seem to defy logical explanation, are often viewed as the language of the universe. Solitary witches remain open to the subtle dance of synchronicities, recognizing them as signs that their intuitive compass is aligned with the greater tapestry of existence.

Shadow Work and Intuition

The shadow, the hidden and often unacknowledged aspects of the self, plays a significant role in intuitive development. Solitary witches engage in shadow work, delving into the depths of their subconscious to uncover and integrate aspects that may hinder intuitive growth. By embracing the shadow, witches align more authentically with their intuitive nature.

Guided Visualization

Guided visualizations become a potent tool in the solitary witch's toolkit for intuitive development. Through visualization exercises, witches explore inner landscapes, meet spirit guides, and attune to the symbols and messages that arise. These journeys into the inner realms deepen the connection to intuitive wisdom.

The Art of Discernment

As intuition unfolds, the solitary witch hones the art of discernment. Not every impulse or feeling is an intuitive insight, and discernment becomes the skill of distinguishing between the noise of the mind and the whispers of intuition. This discernment is cultivated through experience, reflection, and an ongoing relationship with one's intuitive self.

Integrating Intuition into Magical Practice

For the solitary witch, intuition is not a separate facet but an integral part of magical practice. Whether crafting spells, engaging in rituals, or communing with nature, intuition informs every aspect of the witch's craft. Through this integration, intuition becomes a living, breathing companion on the solitary journey.

The Unveiling of Inner Wisdom

In the vast landscape of solitary witchcraft, the development of intuition unveils a reservoir of inner wisdom. Through awareness, connection with nature, meditation, dreamwork, energy perception, and the art of discernment, the solitary witch nurtures the intuitive voice that guides their magical journey. In the dance of shadows and light, the solitary witch becomes a weaver of intuition, crafting a tapestry of insight that enriches every step along the path of magical self-discovery.

CHAPTER TWENTY-EIGHT

ETHICS AND RESPONSIBILITY IN WITCHCRAFT

In the solitary realm of witchcraft, where the practitioner holds the reins of their magical journey, the principles of ethics and responsibility become guiding lights. This chapter delves into the moral compass that shapes the solitary witch's path, exploring the significance of ethical considerations, responsibility to oneself and others, and the interplay between magic and ethical decision-making.

Foundations of Ethical Witchcraft

Understanding the Threefold Law

Central to many ethical frameworks in witchcraft is the concept of the Threefold Law, suggesting that the energy one puts into the world returns threefold. This principle underscores the interconnectedness of actions and their consequences, emphasizing the importance of mindful and responsible magical practices.

Respecting the Wiccan Rede

For those following Wiccan traditions, the Wiccan Rede encapsulates ethical guidelines with the famous line, "An it harm none, do what ye will." This principle encourages witches to consider the potential harm of their actions and urges them to align their magical endeavors with the greater good.

Responsibility to Oneself

The journey of self-discovery in witchcraft often involves introspection and shadow work, confronting and integrating the hidden aspects of oneself. Ethical responsibility to oneself requires the solitary witch to engage in this inner work, fostering self-awareness and personal growth.

Maintaining ethical practices involves setting boundaries, both magically and personally. The solitary witch learns to discern when to say no, when to protect their energy, and when to prioritize self-care. Boundaries are not only a form of self-respect but also a means of preserving one's ethical integrity.

Ethical responsibility includes honoring one's personal truth and authenticity. The solitary witch embraces their unique path, beliefs, and experiences, avoiding the temptation to conform to external expectations. In doing so, they cultivate a sense of integrity that permeates their magical practice.

Responsibility to Others

Consent and Magical Workings

Respecting the autonomy and free will of others is a cornerstone of ethical responsibility. In magical workings, this translates to seeking consent before performing spells or rituals that may affect others. The solitary witch navigates the delicate balance between personal magical intentions and the impact on the wider community.

Avoiding Manipulation

Ethical witchcraft shuns manipulation or coercion. The solitary witch refrains from using magical practices to control or influence others against their will. Instead, they empower themselves and others through collaborative and consensual magical endeavors.

Healing and Assistance

Responsibility to others extends to offering healing and assistance when possible. The solitary witch may use their magical skills to aid others in need, provided it aligns with ethical considerations and respects the autonomy of those seeking assistance.

Navigating Ethical Grey Areas

Love Spells and Consent

Love spells often reside in ethical grey areas, especially concerning the issue of consent. The solitary witch treads carefully, ensuring that any love magic respects the free will and well-being of all involved parties. Ethical responsibility demands a nuanced approach, considering the potential consequences of such workings.

Cursing and Defensive Magic

The use of cursing or defensive magic raises ethical questions for solitary witches. Ethical responsibility involves careful consideration of intent, proportionality, and the potential harm caused. Defensive magic, while acknowledging the right to protect oneself, still necessitates a mindful approach to avoid unnecessary harm.

Environmental and Social Responsibility

Solitary witches often find themselves attuned to the natural world, fostering a sense of environmental responsibility. Ethical witchcraft involves eco-conscious practices, such as sustainable herb harvesting, minimizing environmental impact during rituals, and advocating for the protection of the Earth.

Ethical responsibility extends to social justice and inclusivity in the solitary witch's practice. By embracing diversity, acknowledging cultural sensitivities, and standing against discrimination, the solitary witch contributes to a magical community that values equality and inclusiveness.

Magical Transparency and Accountability

Maintaining a magical journal becomes a tool for ethical transparency and accountability. The solitary witch records spells, rituals, and experiences, reflecting on the outcomes and lessons learned. This practice fosters self-awareness, allowing the witch to observe patterns and adjust their magical approach accordingly.

For those who occasionally participate in group rituals or belong to magical communities, ethical responsibility involves transparent communication and accountability. The solitary witch contributes positively to collective magical endeavors, ensuring that intentions align with ethical principles and promoting an atmosphere of mutual respect.

Dealing with Unintended Consequences

Ethical responsibility includes acknowledging and addressing unintended consequences of magical workings. The solitary witch engages in reflection, assessing the impact of their spells, and, if necessary, takes steps to rectify unintended harm. This ongoing process of course correction is a hallmark of an ethically mindful practitioner.

Teaching and Mentorship

For those who assume mentorship roles, ethical responsibility encompasses guiding with integrity. The solitary witch mentors to empower others, encourage them to explore their unique paths, and emphasizes the importance of ethical considerations in magical practice.

Walking the Ethical Path

In the labyrinth of solitary witchcraft, ethics, and responsibility serve as guiding stars, illuminating the path toward a harmonious and mindful magical practice. The solitary witch, driven by a commitment to ethical principles, navigates the complexities of magical decision-making with awareness, compassion, and a deep respect for the interconnectedness of all things. As they walk the ethical path, the solitary witch becomes a steward of magic, shaping a reality that honors personal truth, respects the autonomy of others, and contributes to the greater well-being of the magical community and the world at large.

Chapter Twenty-Nine

The Wiccan Rede and the Threefold Law

I n the vast tapestry of solitary witchcraft, certain ethical principles stand as pillars, guiding the practitioner on their magical journey. Among these foundational concepts are the Wiccan Rede and the Threefold Law, both revered and contemplated by witches across traditions. This chapter delves into the profound wisdom encapsulated within these principles, exploring their origins, interpretations, and the impact they have on the practice of solitary witchcraft.

The Wiccan Rede: "An it Harm None, Do What Ye Will"

The Wiccan Rede, often condensed to the phrase "An it harm none, do what ye will," embodies a central ethical tenet within modern witchcraft, particularly in Wiccan traditions. This Rede traces its roots to the mid-20th century, with its earliest recorded version found in Doreen Valiente's 1964 poem "The Wiccan Laws." Over time, the Rede has evolved, with different covens and practitioners adapting its language and emphasis to suit their interpretations.

At its core, the Wiccan Rede urges witches to consider the potential harm of their actions and to align their magical endeavors with the greater good. The interpretation of "harm none" can vary among practitioners, ranging from a strict avoidance of any action perceived as harmful to a more nuanced understanding that considers intention, consent, and the greater balance of energies.

For the solitary witch, the Wiccan Rede becomes a guiding principle in ethical decision-making. It prompts introspection and encourages mindfulness in magical practices. The responsibility to weigh the potential consequences of one's actions, ensuring they align with the overarching goal of avoiding harm, becomes a cornerstone of ethical witchcraft.

While the Wiccan Rede sets a moral compass, it also upholds the value of personal autonomy. "Do what ye will" affirms the importance of individual freedom and choice, empowering witches to navigate their unique paths with authenticity. Solitary witches find within the Rede a call to embrace personal responsibility and conscious decision-making in their magical endeavors.

The Threefold Law: "Ever Mind the Rule of Three"

The Threefold Law, often expressed as "Ever mind the rule of three," is an ancient concept that transcends modern Wiccan traditions. Its origins are deeply rooted in mystical and folkloric beliefs that span various cultures. The idea that the energy one puts into the world returns threefold reflects a belief in the interconnectedness of actions and consequences, emphasizing the karmic nature of magical workings.

The Threefold Law suggests that the energy released through magical actions—be they positive or negative—reverberates back to the practitioner with three times the intensity. This interpretation under-scores the concept of reciprocity, encouraging witches to be mind-ful of the intentions and energy they release into the world. While some view this law as a cosmic balancing act, others perceive it as a metaphorical guide for ethical living.

The Threefold Law prompts solitary witches to carefully balance their intentions and the potential outcomes of their magical workings. It calls for a heightened awareness of the energetic ripple effect created by every spell, ritual, or incantation. As a result, witches navigate their magical journeys with a consciousness that extends beyond the immediate moment of spellcasting.

For the solitary witch embracing the Threefold Law, teaching responsibility becomes integral to their practice. Whether mentoring others or engaging in magical communities, witches instill an understanding of the interconnected nature of magical actions. This teaching emphasizes that ethical choices not only impact the individual but reverberate through the wider energetic tapestry of existence.

Harmonizing the Wiccan Rede and the Threefold Law

Complementary Principles

The Wiccan Rede and the Threefold Law are often seen as complementary principles that guide ethical considerations in harmony. The Rede offers a moral directive, prompting witches to evaluate the potential harm of their actions, while the Threefold Law introduces a cosmic perspective on the consequences of those actions. Together, they weave a framework that encourages ethical mindfulness and re-sponsible magical practice.

Solitary witches encounter ethical grey areas where the principles of the Wiccan Rede and the Threefold Law may seem at odds or chal-lenging to interpret. Love spells, defensive magic, or situations where harm seems inevitable require thoughtful consideration. Navigating these grey areas involves an understanding of one's personal ethical code, weighing intentions, and acknowledging the potential impact on the greater web of energies.

Critiques and Alternative Views

While the Wiccan Rede and the Threefold Law resonate deeply with many practitioners, some within the witchcraft community critique these principles. Critics argue that the Rede's emphasis on avoid-ing harm may oversimplify complex ethical considerations, and the Threefold Law's strict karmic interpretation may not align with di-verse belief systems. Solitary witches, in their independent explo-ration, may choose to adopt, adapt, or reinterpret these principles based on their own experiences and evolving understanding.

Solitary witches, recognizing the diversity of magical traditions and ethical perspectives, may choose alternative frameworks that resonate with their personal philosophies. Some draw inspiration from cul-tural, ancestral, or spiritual sources outside Wiccan traditions, con-structing ethical guidelines that align with their unique paths. The exploration of alternative ethical frameworks enriches the tapestry of solitary witchcraft with diverse perspectives.

Guiding Lights on the Magical Path

In the realm of solitary witchcraft, the Wiccan Rede and the Threefold Law emerge as guiding lights, offering ethical considerations and shaping the practitioner's approach to magic. The Rede encourages mindfulness and responsibility, while the Threefold Law introduces a cosmic perspective on the consequences of magical actions. Solitary witches, in their individual journeys, navigate the complexities of these principles, finding resonance, critique, or alternative frameworks that align with their evolving understanding of ethical witchcraft. As they tread the magical path, guided by these principles or others of their choosing, the solitary witch becomes a weaver of intention, crafting a reality that reflects personal integrity, responsibility, and a harmonious relationship with the energies that dance through the threads of existence.

Chapter Thirty

Conclusion: Embracing Your Solitary Path and Reflections on Your Solitary Witchcraft Journey

As you stand at the threshold of this concluding chapter, having traversed the pages of "Solitary Witchcraft for Beginners," it is a moment of reflection and integration. Your solitary witchcraft journey is a unique tapestry woven with the threads of personal discovery, magical exploration, and the wisdom garnered from the pages of this guide. In these concluding words, we delve into the essence of embracing your solitary path, acknowledging the transformative power of reflection, and weaving the insights gained into the ongoing narrative of your magical self.

Embracing Your Solitary Path

The path of the solitary witch is a sacred journey, a solitary dance with the energies that weave through the cosmos. Embracing your solitary path involves recognizing and celebrating the autonomy and authenticity that defines your magical journey. As you navigate the realms of witchcraft, honor the sovereignty of your unique self, acknowledging that your practice is a reflection of your inner truth.

In the realm of solitary witchcraft, personal choice becomes a cornerstone of empowerment. You are the architect of your magical practice, free to choose the traditions, deities, and practices that resonate with your soul. Embrace the diversity of magical expressions, and let your personal choices be guided by intuition, inspiration, and the whispers of the inner self.

Solitude, often feared in a world bustling with noise, becomes a transformative alchemy in the hands of the solitary witch. It is within the sacred space of solitude that you commune with the depths of your own being, explore the uncharted territories of your psyche, and forge a profound connection with the energies that guide your magical endeavors.

As a solitary witch, you are not bound by established traditions unless you choose to be. Create your rituals, forge your traditions, and infuse them with the essence of your personal magic. The freedom to shape your magical landscape allows for innovation, experimentation, and the continual evolution of your craft.

Belief is a fluid river that courses through the landscape of your solitary path. Embrace the ebb and flow of belief systems, allowing them to evolve, adapt, and transform as you traverse the seasons of your magical journey. Your beliefs are not stagnant; they are living expressions that reflect the ever-unfolding nature of your soul.

Reflections on Your Solitary Witchcraft Journey

Reflection is a sacred mirror that unveils the layers of your solitary witchcraft journey. As you gaze into the reflections of your experiences, spells, and rituals, consider the following facets of your magical odyssey.

Throughout your solitary journey, introspection becomes a guiding lantern. Reflect on the facets of self-discovery that have emerged from the depths of your magical practice. What insights have you gleaned about your strengths, vulnerabilities, and the hidden realms of your psyche? How has the mirror of introspection illuminated the contours of your magical self?

In the woven tapestry of spells and rituals, each thread tells a story. Reflect on the spells crafted with intention, the rituals that unfolded under the moonlit sky, and the moments of communion with the sacred. What threads stand out as vibrant expressions of your magical will? How have these spells shaped the energetic landscape of your reality?

As a solitary witch, your encounters with deities, spirits, and unseen forces are intimate and personal. Reflect on the moments of connection, guidance, and revelation that have unfolded on your path. How have these divine and mystical encounters enriched your understanding of the interconnected web of existence? In what ways have you forged alliances with the numinous energies that accompany you on your journey?

Alchemy is the art of transformation, and your journey has witnessed both successes and challenges. Reflect on the alchemy of these experiences. How have challenges been transmuted into opportunities for growth and resilience? In what ways have your successes fueled the flames of inspiration and confidence in your magical abilities?

Nature is a silent mentor, and the elements are the building blocks of your magical foundation. Reflect on the connections forged with the natural world and the elemental forces. How has your relationship with nature deepened? In what ways have the elements served as allies, teachers, and sources of inspiration in your solitary practice?

The journey of a solitary witch often involves the unveiling of intuition—a subtle and guiding force. Reflect on the moments when intuition spoke to you, guiding your magical decisions and shaping the course of your practice. How has the development of intuition enriched your ability to navigate the unseen realms?

While the path of the solitary witch is individual, it is not devoid of community. Reflect on any collaborations, shared rituals, or connections with fellow practitioners. How has the exchange of magical insights and experiences with others enriched your solitary path? In what ways has community contributed to the tapestry of your witchcraft journey?

Continuing the Dance

As this chapter draws to a close, the dance of your solitary witchcraft journey continues. Each step is an invitation to explore, learn, and evolve. Embrace the sacred solitude that defines your path, for within it lies the potential for profound transformation and self-discovery.

Your dialogue with magic is an ongoing conversation. Listen to the whispers of the wind, feel the pulse of the Earth, and commune with the energies that surround you. The language of magic is spoken through symbols, dreams, and the silent spaces between words. Engage in this dialogue with openness and receptivity.

As a solitary witch, embrace the fluidity of your practice. Adapt and grow, allowing your craft to evolve in harmony with the ever-changing seasons of your life. The ability to adapt is a testament to the resilience and creativity inherent in your magical spirit.

The boundaries of your solitary path are expansive, reaching into realms yet undiscovered. Venture beyond the known, explore new territories, and embrace the mysteries that beckon you. The magic of the unseen awaits your discovery, and every step into the unknown is an act of courage and curiosity.

As you continue to weave the threads of your solitary witchcraft journey, consider the wisdom gained from reflection. Allow the insights, lessons, and revelations to become integral threads in the tapestry of your magical self. Each thread contributes to the rich narrative of your evolving story.

Closing the Grimoire

In the closing of this grimoire, may the wisdom contained within these pages serve as a lantern to illuminate your solitary path. Embrace the solitude that is both sanctuary and crucible and let the reflections on your journey be a source of inspiration. Your solitary witchcraft journey is a dance with the sacred, a symphony of magical expressions, and a testament to the ever-unfolding nature of your unique self. As you step into the continuing chapters of your magical life, may the threads of your solitary path weave a tapestry that resonates with authenticity, wisdom, and the timeless magic that dwells within you.

Chapter Thirty-One
RESOURCES

In the journey of solitary witchcraft, knowledge is a potent ally, and resources serve as guideposts along the enchanted path. This chapter unfolds as a repository of invaluable resources, offering a tapestry woven with books, websites, and communities that will illuminate, inspire, and deepen your connection to the craft.

Books to Illuminate Your Path:

- **"Solitary Witch" by Silver RavenWolf:** A comprehensive guide for the solitary practitioner, this book covers a range of topics, from rituals and spells to the fundamentals of Wiccan traditions.

- **"Witch: Unleashed. Untamed. Unapologetic." by Lisa Lister:** This empowering read delves into embracing the witch within, encouraging authenticity and reclaiming personal power.

- **"The Modern Witchcraft Spell Book" by Skye Alexan-

der: A spellbook catering to modern witches, providing a diverse collection of spells, charms, and rituals suitable for solitary practice.

- **"Drawing Down the Moon" by Margot Adler:** A classic exploration of modern pagan and witchcraft movements, offering insights into the history and diverse practices within the craft.

- **"The Green Witch" by Arin Murphy-Hiscock:** Focused on natural magic and herbalism, this book guides the solitary witch in connecting with the energies of the earth.

- **"The Witch's Book of Self-Care" by Arin Murphy-Hiscock:** Exploring the intersection of self-care and witchcraft, this resource offers practical rituals and insights to nurture the mind, body, and spirit.

- **"The Complete Book of Witchcraft" by Raymond Buckland:** A foundational guide covering the basics of witchcraft, rituals, and magical tools, suitable for both beginners and those looking to deepen their practice.

- **"Scott Cunningham's Encyclopedia of Magical Herbs" by Scott Cunningham:** A valuable resource for herbal magic, providing insights into the magical properties of various herbs and plants.

- **"The Witch's Shield" by Christopher Penczak:** Focused on psychic self-defense and protection, this book equips the solitary witch with tools to navigate the energetic realms.

- **"Cunningham's Book of Shadows" by Scott Cunning-

ham: A practical guide to creating and maintaining a Book of Shadows, tailored for the solitary practitioner.

Online Resources for Continued Learning:

- **Witchvox (witchvox.com):** An online community and resource hub, Witchvox connects witches, pagans, and magical practitioners around the world. It offers articles, events, and a directory of local groups.

- **The Witch's Voice (thewitchestoolbox.com):** A website dedicated to providing a variety of tools and resources for witches, including spellwork, correspondences, and articles on various magical topics.

- **Sacred Texts (sacred-texts.com):** An extensive collection of esoteric texts, folklore, and ancient manuscripts, offering a wealth of knowledge for those interested in delving into historical and traditional aspects of witchcraft.

- **Llewellyn's Spell-A-Day (llewellyn.com/spelladay):** A daily source of spell ideas and magical inspiration from the renowned publisher Llewellyn, offering practical rituals for different occasions.

- **The Wild Hunt (wildhunt.org):** A news site focused on modern pagan, Heathen, and polytheist communities, providing insightful articles and updates on the intersection of religion, culture, and activism.

- **Witches & Pagans Magazine (witchesandpagans.com**

): A magazine exploring contemporary pagan and magical practices, featuring articles, interviews, and reviews relevant to the witchcraft community.

- **The Pagan Federation (paganfed.org):** An organization supporting pagans, witches, and druids, offering resources, events, and networking opportunities for those on diverse pagan paths.

- **The Astrology Podcast (theastrologypodcast.com):** For witches interested in astrology, this podcast provides in-depth discussions and interviews on various astrological topics.

- **The Witchery (thewitchery.ca):** An online platform offering courses and resources on witchcraft, magic, and divination, fostering a supportive community for solitary practitioners.

- **YouTube - Harmony Nice (youtube.com/user/harmonyNice):** A popular YouTuber and solitary witch, Harmony shares insights into her personal practices, spellwork, and experiences, offering a visual and accessible approach to witchcraft.

Local and Online Communities:

- **Meetup (meetup.com):** An online platform facilitating the formation of local and virtual witchcraft and pagan groups, offering opportunities to connect with like-minded individuals.

- **Witchy Facebook Groups:** Joining Facebook groups dedicated to witchcraft, such as "Witches of the World" or "Solitary Witches," provides a space for sharing experiences, asking questions, and building a supportive community.

- **Instagram Witchcraft Community:** Engaging with the vibrant and diverse witchcraft community on Instagram allows you to connect with fellow witches, share your own practices, and gain inspiration from others.

- **Discord Servers:** Numerous Discord servers cater to witchcraft and pagan discussions, providing a real-time platform for chatting, sharing resources, and participating in community events.

- **Local Occult or Metaphysical Shops:** Visiting local occult or metaphysical shops can connect you with the broader magical community in your area. These shops often host events, classes, and gatherings.

- **Pagan Pride Events:** Attending Pagan Pride events in your region can be an enriching experience, offering opportunities to meet practitioners, attend workshops, and explore diverse aspects of pagan and witchcraft traditions.

- **Witchcraft Conventions:** Participating in witchcraft conventions, whether in person or virtual, provides a platform for learning from experts, connecting with vendors, and immersing yourself in the wider witchcraft community.

Nourishing Your Witchcraft Journey

As you embark on or deepen your journey into solitary witchcraft, these resources become beacons of guidance, sources of inspiration, and portals to community. Let them be companions on your magical odyssey, supporting you in the continual exploration of the sacred realms. May your solitary path be adorned with the wisdom gleaned from books, the connectivity fostered by online resources, and the warmth of community, both local and virtual. In the dance of the solitary witch, may these resources illuminate your way, empowering you to craft a magical practice that resonates with the authenticity of your unique soul.

About the Author

Willow De Witte is an enchanting soul who finds her home, love, and joy in the breathtaking landscapes of the great state of Colorado. Nestled amid majestic mountains and sprawling plains, Willow embraces the beauty of nature as an integral part of her spiritual journey.

With her vast and loving family, Willow has always valued the connections that bind us. Her journey through life has taken her through the vibrant tapestry of experiences in both bustling cities and serene rural areas, enriching her perspective on the diverse landscapes of human existence.

A seasoned practitioner of the mystical arts, Willow has been immersed in the world of tarot for over four decades. Her tarot practice serves as a compass, guiding her and others through the intricate paths of life with wisdom and insight. Alongside tarot, she has dedicated three decades to the study and practice of witchcraft, weaving magic into the fabric of her existence.

In the hustle and bustle of life, Willow seeks solace and tranquility where she can find it. Her connection to the natural world, coupled with her spiritual practices, allows her to cultivate a sense of peace amidst the chaos. Whether drawing energy from the city lights or the quiet serenity of rural landscapes, Willow embraces the duality of her experiences.

As an author, Willow De Witte shares her wealth of knowledge and experiences in the realms of tarot and witchcraft. Her writings reflect not only her expertise but also the genuine passion she holds for these ancient and mystical arts. Through her words, Willow invites readers into a world where magic, intuition, and the profound wisdom of the tarot converge to illuminate the journey of self-discovery.

Join Willow as she opens the door to her magical realm, inviting you to explore the realms of tarot, witchcraft, and the harmonious dance between the spiritual and the earthly in her writings.